Soul Talk

VOL. 2

Soul Talk
VOL. 2
SOUL-STIRRING STORIES OF PEOPLE WHO LET GO AND LET GOD

CHERYL POLOTE-WILLIAMSON

SOUL TALK, VOL. 2
Published by Purposely Created Publishing Group™
Copyright © 2018 Cheryl Polote-Williamson
All rights reserved.

No part of this book may be reproduced, distributed or transmitted in any form by any means, graphics, electronics, or mechanical, including photocopy, recording, taping, or by any information storage or retrieval system, without permission in writing from the publisher, except in the case of reprints in the context of reviews, quotes, or references.

Printed in the United States of America

ISBN: 978-1-949134-39-1

Special discounts are available on bulk quantity purchases by book clubs, associations and special interest groups. For details email:
sales@publishyourgift.com
or call (888) 949-6228.

For information logon to:
www.PublishYourGift.com

Dedication

This book is dedicated to every person who is still having trouble "letting go and letting God."

In Him,
Cheryl Polote-Williamson

Table of Contents

Ignoring Pain Will Not Make It Go Away
Dr. Terry Richardson 1

Into the Oceans Deep
Alicia Simon 11

I Shall Live
Debbie Chandler 21

Choices that Challenged, Changes that Conquered:
All in Black and White
Kymberli Williams 31

Chasing Invisible Smoke
Cynthia Fox Everett 41

When Morning Tarries
Christine Norman 49

The Cycle of Generational Dysfunction
Kimberly Solomon 59

My Brokenness: His Undying Love!
Sharon L. Graves 69

Abandoned, Molested, and Abused Before My Awakening
Sheila Malloy-Hall 79

The Unthinkable That Happened
Laquita Hogan 89

Self-Love: Loving Yourself Is Seeing Yourself the Way God Sees You!
Sonya Scott 99

His Sins, My Journey
Windi Floyd Reynolds 107

Training Day
DeNesha Manning 115

If You FIGHT, the Devil Can't Win
Winifred "Teddi" Jones 125

Forgiveness
LaShonda Davison 133

Trusting God Through the Process
LaVerne M. Perlie 141

My Truth but God's Plan
Katherine Romar 151

The Awakening
Dionne Selby 161

I Knew it Was Time to JUMPP
Dana Campbell 169

Stop Cheering and Get in the Game!
Angela T. Kinnel 179

Thankful for Choices—I Choose to Live!
Monica Monk Oliver 187

Sources 197
About the Authors 199

Ignoring Pain Will Not Make it Go Away

DR. TERRY RICHARDSON

"Heal me, O LORD, and I shall be healed; save me, and I shall be saved: for thou art my praise."

—Jeremiah 17:14 (KJV)

For years, I ignored a deep childhood hurt. The pain from my experience resulted in a lifelong struggle of negative self-perception. For four decades I limped through life with an open, yet hidden wound. I functioned well in life, but in constant pain. One day, God unveiled my pain in such a way that I was forced to face it directly. It was this confrontation that delivered me from a lifetime of struggle and validated my soul's purpose.

Life has a way of dishing out unexpected and unwanted challenges. Oftentimes, these challenges are necessary to shape and catapult us into our destiny. It can take years of toting around unnecessary pain before realizing God is able to use our pain to shape us into who He meant for us to become. When painfully devastating moments occur in life, it can be impossible to view such experiences as crafted circumstances designed to reveal our soul's purpose. Today, many believe it's illogical to think pain and destiny have anything to do with each other. Yet, they do. I learned that our pain can be a sign of destiny in the making. Here's a pivotal question for anyone hiding and lugging around hurt from years ago. After hiding and ignoring your pain, are you better off for carrying it around for so long? In other words, does your pain still have the power to rob you of your joy in life? My friend, hiding and ignoring pain won't make it go away no more than dressing it up to look good will take away its crippling effects on your soul.

When faced with anxiety, 1 Peter 5:7 (KJV) encourages us to cast our cares upon God, "for he careth for you." As I reminisce about parts of my childhood, I was unable to find a road map that would lead me to reconcile the hurt and pain I experienced as a boy. Like so many others, wishing my pain away didn't work as a practical step in confronting it or removing it altogether.

My pain began the day my dad referred to me as "ugly and dumb." Don't get me wrong, my father was a good man. Granted, he faced a few challenges that I never understood growing up as a boy. While those challenges barred heavy on me, my mom, and my four brothers, for the most part dad was a good man who loved his family. However, from that moment of my boyhood on, my soul became wounded, and I struggled with deep pains of rejection and hate toward my dad along with crippling effects of a negative self-image. For years, this pain robbed me of a positive self-identity.

Father Wounds

In his work, *33 The Series: Authentic Manhood A Man and His Story*, Dr. Robert Lewis refers to this type of pain as "Father Wounds"—the intentional or unintentional pain caused by our fathers. Many are carrying around unreconciled father wounds (or mother wounds) from decades ago. The only purpose of those wounds is to cause us pain and stop us from reaching our God-given purpose.

Words have a way of cutting deeper than any metal or steel object ever could. Being described as ugly and dumb was like venom entering my psyche. I translated this to mean I didn't belong and didn't measure up to others. Those words left a gaping hole in my heart. For years, they kept me from believing in myself.

Do you know that we can have a sense of where we need to be, yet be unable to reconcile how to get there? Even while serving as a senior pastor, I found myself unable to move beyond the pain of my father wounds and its effects.

Again, ignoring pain will not cause the pain to cease. Instead of addressing my hurts, I learned to mask my struggle with unforgiveness and my low self-image from persons closest to me—my wife, children, and congregation.

If unresolved hurt from past relationships is a challenge for you, understand that unresolved hurt develops into resentment and bitterness. Here's another pivotal question for you to ask yourself. What pain from your past is keeping you from your future?

Confrontation with Pain

My 40-year-old pain was finally confronted one afternoon during a conversation with my esteemed professor and mentor, Dr. Warren Dennis. "Terry," he asked, "what pain from your past is keeping you from performing on the level you are capable?" His words were so penetrating that upon hearing the question, I literally began to cry buckets of uncontrollable tears. I was unable to contain myself. For me it was a question of lost identity. The core of my soul had been shaken by such a simple question. Deep within my soul, I was tired of the up and down roller coaster of hiding behind low-esteem and hurt. I was trapped inside of myself. I was tired of playing this game.

I helplessly stood there crying. Dr. Dennis broke his silence by suggesting I write my memoirs. Honestly, it was awkward. Two weeks passed before I finally stopped crying and drummed up the courage to begin writing. I had been clueless of the true effect and damage carrying pain around so long had on me. Writing my memoirs meant revisiting that pain.

The idea of revisiting my past frightened me. But, at least I would not go it alone. I told God I needed Him to walk with me on this journey. He instructed me not to leap back into my past, but to walk my story in reverse. I could not see Him but felt His presence as I began writing. We set out and started walking my life in reverse, beginning with the very day I started writing. God led me on a spiritual journey down through the seasons of my adulthood, young adult, teenage, and boyhood years. We finally ended up in my childhood bedroom. Growing up, my childhood bedroom was a place of solitude, escape, and security. I thought it was funny God paused there of all places. Mine was a typical suburban bedroom.

Tell Me What You See

As I stood in the center of the room, God said, "Tell me what you see." Immediately, I began to call out the items in my room. Everything was in place just as I remembered it. God said, "Now tell me what you missed." Puzzled by the question, my eyes meticulously probed the room a second time. After a thorough and careful sweep with my eyes, I convincingly told myself there was nothing I missed.

You Missed Me

Before I could offer God my answer, He offered me a revelation, "You missed Me." He said, "I was there the entire time. The reason it (your wound) didn't killed you is because I told the devil, this far and no further." Wow! Immediately mixed feelings of loneliness, solitude, and guilt lifted from my soul. I felt both surprised and relieved.

As an adolescent, I received Jesus Christ as my Savior in this room. I had come to trust and believe He would never leave me nor forsake me. Yet, God was making it perfectly clear, I had missed His presence. Throughout the critical moments in my life, I had missed His abiding presence. I hadn't fully understood He was always present desiring me to reach out to Him.

I felt the pain I was harboring for over 40 years melt away. For the first time in my life, I heard a father's words of love and embrace. They were words from my Father in Heaven. The hole in my soul was beginning to fill with God's affirmation of me. He was telling me that He cared enough to fight off every crippling enemy from my life.

Oftentimes growing up I'd fantasize about what it would be like to receive a cheer from my earthly dad. I loathed the fact that I had not been affirmed by such an important person in my life. Over the years, I wondered how far a word of support would have taken me. What could one word of affirmation have set into motion?

God telling me He was there with me the entire time was colossal. It blessed me to know God hadn't abandoned me during that difficult time in my life. He helped me put that part of my life into proper perspective. God will never abandon those who are His.

Your Father Has Pain

In no uncertain terms, the next revelation God shared with me would shatter me, heal me, and unveil what He had been up to all along. "It wasn't your fault," He told me. "You did nothing wrong," God said. "Your father said and did those things because he was hurting." Instantly the drapes of darkness were drawn back from my eyes and heart. For the first time, an incredible brightness replaced the dark thoughts I had toward my father. God allowed me to see and feel the hidden pain nestled deep inside the heart of my dad. For the first time, it began to make sense.

God revealed how my father had been a victim of his own pain. God recalled a boyhood memory I was too young to understand at the time concerning the dynamics of how my dad lost his job after attempting to sue his employer for job discrimination. He was then blackballed. He spent all he had defending his case and lost. Not too long after losing, our family began experiencing the impact of his pain.

Soul Healing is Soul Deliverance

Understanding that my father was broken by his own pain broke the power of unforgiveness over my life. Immediately I felt a release come over me. No longer could a memory trigger hate in my heart. After decades of battling the effects of hurt, my soul was finally delivered. No longer was I feeling less than everyone around me and I began loving my dad again. My hurt had become my testimony.

In my heart I questioned why God had not healed my soul years ago. His answer to me was that I had been praying for strength, not healing. Each time I asked for strength to forgive, God granted me the strength I needed for that moment. In an oversight, I never asked God to remove all the hurt from my heart; thus, I had unnecessarily lived in a place of pain most of my life. While I was looking for momentary strength to love, God wanted to heal my soul from hurts relentless grip.

Destiny and a Divine Plan

Just when I thought God was finished, He said to me, "I allowed all that happened to you to make you the leader you are today." I was speechless once again. God had already revealed how He was present during the most painful time of my life, covering me while keeping the hurt in life from crushing me. He had also allowed me to see behind the curtain wall of pain dad carried, and delivered me from my struggle with unforgiveness. Now, God was showing me my worth in His plan of redemption. My sense of self-worth that had been hidden beneath years of living with a wounded soul. I had no idea it was God's plan to use my hurt. Romans 8:28 says, "And we know that all things work together for good to those who love God, to those who are the called according to His purpose" (NKJV). This Scripture has become real in my life.

God then took me into the air where He showed me an aerial view of a beach with a trail of footprints stretching from one end of the beach to the other. Like the encounter in my room, I was unable to see God, but I could feel His presence all around me. I thought to myself, "Now that He has revealed that He used everything in my life to prepare me to be His leader, He is now showing me how He was there to keep me over the journey of my life."

Able to read my thoughts, God responded by saying, "Those are not your footprints, they are Mine. I carried you." There is a popular poem authored by Mary Stevenson entitled, "Footprints in the Sand." In her vision, God walked alongside her on a seashore where at times she noticed the set of footprints went from two to one over the difficult moments in her journey. God showed Stevenson that He carried her during the most challenging times of her life. However, God wasn't revealing to me He was carrying me during the most difficult time of my life. Instead, God showed me that He had been my strength during my struggle with unforgiveness and low self-esteem. It was Him who cared for and fathered me throughout my life. I was never alone, but always valued, loved, and celebrated. When my earthly father was unable to express the love I needed due to his own pain, God reached down to love me and give me the strength I needed.

SOUL REFLECTION:
God used the unexpected pain of my life to shape me. I am a witness of His power to reconcile and deliver His children from the depths of pain, hopelessness, and despair. Hiding my pain tore me apart on the inside. It affected almost every part of my identity. Today, I shout with the voice of triumph. I pray you learn to trust God enough to give Him your pain. Ignoring it doesn't make it go away. Trust God by letting Him use your pain to launch you into your purpose. Your destiny is waiting for you. I have spoken in front of thousands of people to declare God can take your pain and turn it into praise. He can take your soul-pain and turn it into your soul-purpose.

Into the Oceans Deep

ALICIA SIMON

"Jumping out of the boat, Peter walked on the water to Jesus. But when he looked down at the waves churning beneath his feet, he lost his nerve and started to sink. He cried, 'Master, save me!' Jesus didn't hesitate. He reached down and grabbed his hand. Then he said, 'Faint-heart, what got into you?' The two of them climbed into the boat, and the wind died down."

—Matthew 14:29-32 (MSG)

Sun-kissed Beaches

There's nothing more relaxing than a day at the beach. The warmth of the sun, the cool breeze coming off the ocean, the golden specks of sand between my toes, that is my happy place.

On September 18, 1992, I gave birth to a beautiful baby boy. I was seventeen years old and scared. I had no idea how to raise this tiny little human; I only knew that I wanted to be a good mother. Regardless of what I had done, God chose me to be his mother. I wasn't going to mess this up. For the first time in my life, I felt called to something bigger than myself. I hesitate to consider the course of my life if he was never born. I heard the Lord whisper to me, "Alicia, because you are in Christ Jesus you are no longer condemned. What you did was your mistake; this baby is My miracle. I have plans for you. I have plans for your son. Justin will do a mighty work for me one day." God gave me a second chance. Holding Justin in my arms for the first time was like an endless day on a beautiful beach.

Along the Shore

I love to hear the sound of waves crashing against the shore. It's mind numbing. Sometimes I leave the water running in the sink and take myself on an imaginary trip to the beach. What I don't like as much is walking along the beach too close to the shoreline. Warm and cozy is my comfort zone. Along the shoreline, the ocean inches closer and closer inland, sweeping its frothy, chilled waves upon the shore, chasing after my bare toes.

Several years passed since the day I first held my tiny newborn in my arms. My son was doing well in school. His personality was electric. He could light up a room as soon as he walked in. Bright, beautiful, and full of laughter. I read Scripture and sang songs to my baby daily. My favorite was my own personal remix, "You are my Sonshine, my only Sonshine. You make me happy when skies are gray. Justin, I love you, I really love you. God, please don't take my Sonshine away." He and I were inseparable.

On December 28, 1996, Justin's father was shot and killed. I was devastated. Why would God allow this to happen? I felt alone. I felt no one truly understood my pain. I wanted to go inward and return to familiar dark places. I had only one hope to cling to—God's promise to help me be a good mom.

Soon after Justin's father died, I began making plans to move out and raise my son on my own. Everything was going well, until my final semester in college when I was offered an academic fellowship in another state. While I was nervous to do something so grand, I got excited for a new adventure. As I redrafted my plans, I felt a glimmer of hope. A song was returning to my heart. However, my parents, my son, and pretty much everyone around me was not as excited. They were proud of my offer, but convinced that my decision to take Justin with me was the worst thing I could possibly do. Justin and I had known only this small town in the south all of our lives. They reasoned it would be too much for me to handle. I tried to ignore the unsolicited advice, but for the first time, I doubted my ability to care for my son. After all, my parents had always been there, and they love him just as much as I do. Then there was Justin, begging me to let him stay. This was his home. How could I take him away? Regrettably, I packed only myself and headed North. Michigan was hard; I faced lots of challenges and temptations. As hard as it was, it was also a turning point for me. In the middle of a spring snowstorm, near the end of March 1998, my faith was challenged head on. I was given a choice by God—live a fulfilled life in Christ or die a slow death in sin. With only a tiny morsel of faith remaining, I chose Christ. Walking along the shoreline is definitely not one of my favorite pastimes, but I endure the agony of the cold waves wrapped around my ankles because they always leave behind gems from the ocean—a unique shell, a beautiful stone, a lost treasure, a renewed faith.

Swept Up by the Ocean's Current

Have you ever walked out into the ocean, away from the shore? I don't do it often, but when I do, I have to prepare myself. My feet are planted deep into the sand so that I'm not swept up by the ocean's current. I stand firm, I brace myself. I think I'm ready...

By the time I married my husband on May 13, 2006, Justin was 13 years old. No matter how many times I tried, I could never bring myself to disrupt his seemingly perfect life for him to live with me. I was starting to realize there weren't many years left for us to be together again. In December of 2007, despite my fears, we transitioned Justin into our home. Finally, we were together again.

Our family grew quickly. By the end of 2013, we added three sons and one daughter. Our family was not perfect, but it was good. We had the typical trials in our marriage—communication, intimacy, differences of opinion, and finances. We had trials parenting a teenager, three toddlers, and a baby. Justin was now in college, had acknowledged his call to preach, and had a son of his own. We all had our set of trials, but for the most part, life was good.

Late one night near the end of summer in 2014, I was startled awake by the ring of my cell phone. I jumped up quickly to answer, thinking it was my son. It was my father.

I was concerned. He never called so late. I barely said hello and he hurriedly asked when was the last time I'd talked to Justin. I told him that he'd called that morning to wish my husband a happy birthday, but I hadn't spoken to him since. Now, I'm sitting straight up in my bed, waiting impatiently for the punchline. He said it... "The US Marshals just left looking for Justin." I screamed! "Why? What happened? Is he okay?" My father tried his best to calmly articulate what was happening, but my hearing was clouded by my own sobs and my mother wailing in the background. My husband, realizing something was wrong, awoke from his sleep and drew close to me. After what seemed like a lifetime, I finally processed what my father had said. "Justin is a suspect in a triple homicide." So many questions poured out of my mouth, but my father didn't have any answers. It took everything in me, between the gasps for air, to articulate to my husband what my father was saying. The next several seconds, minutes, hours, days are embossed in my memory so deeply that even today, even as I write, I can feel every single emotion that I felt in every single second of that time. If it weren't for my husband, my brother, and close friends who walked through those initial days with me, I don't know how I would have made it. To relive those moments brings almost as much pain today as if I were experiencing it all for the first time. What I remember most is wishing with all my heart that every breath I took was my last. The pain was so deep; I wanted to stop existing. In the days to come, my son was located, arrested, booked, and charged with capital murder. My world was shattered. In what seemed like an instant, my life was changed forever. The thought of my son spending the rest of his days behind bars and me living life without my Sonshine was enough to cast a dark shadow over my heart. On August 2, 2014, at 11:30 p.m., I went to bed a good mother to five beautiful children. On August 3, 2014, at 1:34 a.m., I woke up a murder's momma. In this dark moment, I willfully stand where the shore ends, and the ocean begins. I see the waves coming. I rush into the ocean. The swell grows taller and taller, stronger and stronger with every wave. In this moment, I wish for the most enormous wave to swallow me up and carry me away, never returning.

Wave After Wave Crashing Over Me

The next three years were the toughest times I ever faced. I had to learn how to be a wife to my husband and a mother to my four small children, while continuing to love and support my oldest, now incarcerated, son. I did the best I could to be happy and hopeful, but I was dying a slow death inside. Not only was my son in jail physically, but he seemed to be locked away spiritually and mentally. I couldn't connect to him. I didn't understand what had happened; we were so close. I wanted to believe that this was all a mistake, a nightmare. I wanted to believe that he was innocent and would soon return home. There was so much going on in and around me. I was thrust into the deep of the ocean and the waves were unyielding. They kept coming, wave after wave, crashing over me.

On April 29, 2017, at approximately 1:15 p.m., my sweet baby boy pled guilty to capital murder and was handed a sentence of life without parole. I walked out of that courtroom heavy but hopeful. It could have been a death sentence. My son will live. The Lord whispered, "I am not finished with you and I am not finished with Justin. Be courageous, take my hand. Come! Walk on water with me."

How to Walk on Water When Waves are Crashing All Around You

- Maybe you've been through some tough times in life. Your story may be different, but the pain is just as heavy. When the waves of life overwhelm you, do you get distracted and take your eyes off Jesus? Or do you look up and reach for Jesus' hand? Here are a few ways God helped me keep my eyes on Jesus and stay above the waves.
- **Check Your Vision**—Like Peter, amidst my storms, I often took my eyes off Jesus and focused on the waves around me. Every time I felt myself sinking, Jesus sent little reminders of His presence—a Scripture or a sermon, the comfort of a friend. I remind you of Jesus' invitation in Matthew 11:28 (KJV), "Come unto me, all ye that labour and are heavy laden, and I will give you rest." When the waters are calm, take time to dive deep into the Word and it may be easier to hear and see Jesus when the storms begin to rage.
- **Laugh Out Loud (LOL)**—Proverbs 15:13 (MSG) says, "A cheerful heart brings a smile to your face; a sad heart makes it hard to get through the day." I

never had a warning before the feelings of depression and hopelessness would overwhelm me. Yet, on my darkest days, I found a way to laugh. I'd call a funny friend (thank God I have lots of them), or I'd post on social media and ask my online friends to tell me jokes or post a funny gif. And my favorite was lying in bed covered in tears... tears of sorrow that had been turned into tears of laughter as I watched ridiculous comedy shorts on my phone. What makes you laugh so hard your belly aches? That very thing may be just what you need in times of sorrow.

- **Serve Others**—2 Corinthians 1:4 (NIV) says, "who comforts us in all our troubles, so that we can comfort those in any trouble with the comfort we ourselves receive from God." One day I felt so low that I forced myself to share my pain on social media and post a song that was ministering to my heart in that moment. That song was "Oceans" by Hillsong. The response was unbelievable. So many people were hurting in silence and were commenting to say, "Thank you for sharing your story." Those comments gave me an outlet, a place to pour myself out for someone else. Has God called you to share your pain in a way that makes you uncomfortable? Consider that call as His way of using your story to comfort someone else. Watch lives begin to transform as you obey and share.
- **Find Healthy Ways to Manage the Emotions**—I wish I could say I never had outbursts of anger and I never sunk so deeply in sorrow that some days my

husband had to manage the kids and home without me. Or that I never drove down the street thinking, "I could end all this pain right now with one flick of my wrist." Depression was real, and it was hitting me at the core. Some days were worse than others. But God had a prescription just for me in Isaiah 61:3 (KJV), "To appoint unto them that mourn in Zion, to give unto them beauty for ashes, the oil of joy for mourning, the garment of praise for the spirit of heaviness..." Even though I'd been using, selling, and educating others on essential oils for several years, it took me a little while to admit my emotional imbalances and begin to figure out which products would help me manage. God had already equipped me with what I needed to carry me through, and He helped me choose several essential oils and supplements and create a regimen that nourished my body internally. Have you considered using natural alternatives to help manage your emotions? You don't have to suffer in silence anymore.

SOUL REFLECTION:
When you find yourself in the middle of the ocean, overwhelmed by the waves of life, remember this from Psalm 91:15 (KJV), "He shall call upon me, and I will answer him: I will be with him in trouble; I will deliver him, and honour him."—God

I Shall Live

DEBBIE CHANDLER

"I shall not die, but live, and declare the works of the Lord."
—Psalm 118:17 (KJV)

As the blood rolled down my arm (only I would pause in the middle of a botched suicide attempt to take in the fascination of the moment), I realized I had never seen an actual tendon or ligament before, even though at the time I worked as a medical assistant. The tendon resembles an off-white rubber band, surrounded by dark pink fasciae and muscle tissue, similar to the drawings you see in the doctor's office or biology class. I know this because I got a firsthand look into my body when I slit my left wrist in a suicide attempt. It did not matter how much force I used to slice the band-like tissue beneath my skin, it would not separate, pop, or break. Although there was much blood from slicing through to the dermis layers of skin, that was not sufficient for me at that moment, I was gunning for the main line. I knew if I were able to cut my ligaments, veins, and arteries, surely, I would bleed out and death would follow.

As I continued, in the midst of a bloody mess in my room, I began to grow weary and frustrated because after a while the blood flow was slowing. I realized the knife would not cut what appeared to be, again, a rubber band. Somehow, and I know now it was the Holy Spirit, I have a moment of clarity and realize what I am doing. I toss the knife away from me, get up off my bedroom floor, and begin to walk slowly through the hallway and into my living room where my brother was asleep on my couch. With heavy tears streaming down my face, I tapped his shoulder and quietly said, "Brother... look." Still groggy from his sleep, he says, "Look at what?" I motioned for him to look down at my wrist. I was in too much emotional pain to speak as the blood continued down my arm and hand. It was obvious he was horrified by the open gash and all he could say was, "Debbie, NO!" Trying to hold back his tears, he asked me, "Why?" and I had no answer. I simply sat weeping as he called an ambulance, sat with me, held me, and said nothing until they came.

I wish I could say this is the only time I flirted with death; however, it was not. Ever since I was 10 years old, I wanted to escape the pain I lived with. Over the years, the compounded pain from molestations, domestic violence, abortions, and spousal rape was too much to bear. At the time of that particular suicide attempt, I was clueless and unaware that the horrific acts against my body were the culprit for all of my pain. I honestly did not want to kill myself nor did I want to die, I only wanted the pain, guilt, and shame I lived with to stop. At that time in my life, I believed there was no other option but death.

My first attempt at suicide was at the tender age of fourteen, after a horrible act of domestic violence committed against me by one of my older brothers. It was a violation that was surreal and unimaginable. I was in the house one evening when he came home in a rage. Realizing I was there alone, he physically and verbally abused me for approximately three hours. The act exacerbated the already constant feelings of shame and guilt that shadowed my daily existence. And now, I lived in fear for my life; and it was not false evidence appearing real. What I experienced daily was legitimate anguish that I lived exposed to a young man that could harm me at his will. With madness running rampant inside of me and feeling like I had no one to turn to, I took an entire bottle of vitamins. Yes, vitamins. The only result was about 24 hours of severe nausea and vomiting. I knew after that pills, well at least vitamins, may not be the way to go.

The dichotomy of it all is the very room where my brother assaulted me is also the same room where two years prior, when I was 12 years old, God taught me how to read and understand His written Word. God was preparing me for what the enemy prepared for me.

I received a brown Gideon Bible from my mother. I did not want it, nor did I receive it well from her; yet, she insisted with force that I "must" read it. She had just come back from a trip to the Pocono Mountains Resort in Pennsylvania. She gave my siblings and I little trinkets and t-shirts, but I am the only one she insisted must have that Bible. Although my mom was Catholic, we did not attend mass or church, so I did not get why she would want me to have the Bible. I was furious and mumbled under my breath, "I don't want that book, it's brown and not pretty at all." But I knew, for some reason, this was not the moment to disobey and back-talk my mom.

I took the brown book, went to my room, slammed my door, sat on my bed pouting, opened it, and began reading. As I browsed through it, immediately I became hooked and couldn't put it down. I did not know it would speak to me so personally. The easiest place for me to start was in the sections that matched my emotions and situations with a Scripture. Not many people detected that I was very lonely, sad, angry, and that I felt abandoned; so, I found solace in the Word of God. At that time, my go-to sections were:

When you are lonely read... Psalm 25:16 (NIV)—"Turn to me and be gracious to me, for I am lonely and afflicted."

When you are sad read... 1 Peter 5:7 (ESV)—"casting all your anxieties on him, because he cares for you."

When you are angry read... James 1:19-20 (KJV)—"Wherefore, my beloved brethren, let every man be swift to hear, slow to speak, slow to wrath: For the wrath of man worketh not the righteousness of God."

When you feel abandoned read... Psalm 27:10 (NKJV)—"When my father and my mother forsake me, Then the Lord will take care of me."

Without knowing much of anything about church, I began to love this brown Gideon Bible. The more I read, the more I wanted to read. It spoke to me and I wanted more. Many days, I could not wait to get home from school just to be in the presence of what I felt when I read it. At that time, I had no idea it was Jesus teaching me and that later He would send the Holy Spirit to comfort me throughout the rest of my life. I always felt such peace and safety when reading it as if

I was in the company of a friend. It absolutely was a book I understood with ease, and still is to this day.

At fourteen, I started attending church regularly. I loved everything church represented, especially the safety away from home, the food, and the fellowship. The only thing that left me confused was the thought that everyone who went to church read the Bible. I was wrong and hurt the day I said to my church friends, "Hey, let's read the Bible." They responded by laughing at me and saying, "Girl, don't nobody want to read the Bible!" Both shocked and embarrassed, it is then that I began to struggle with my identity. I didn't know exactly where I fit in or what to do because outside of Sunday service or weekly Bible study there was no anchor for me to hold on to.

Struggling with fitting in became an increasing burden that often left me wrestling with what is wrong and right according to the Word of God versus the example of living from my family and the world around me. That anguish always took me to James 1:8, "A double minded man is unstable in all his ways." I lived with heavy guilt knowing what I read in God's Word was true yet still having a challenging time applying it to my everyday life when needed.

What I know now is I was not strong enough, on my own, to combat the horrific temptations of suicide. I was always fearful. I lived controlled by a spirit of fear and anxiety that made me fearful of anything I attempted or desired to accomplish (especially if it caused me to come out of my introverted shell). However, I still knew that if I turned to the Word of God there would be another Scripture to live by, and there was.

When fearful read... 2 Timothy 1:7 (KJV)—"For God hath not given us the spirit of fear; but of power, and of love, and of a sound mind."

I would repeatedly read this Scripture and cry because even though I knew it had to be true, I still felt separated from Jesus. That lack of faith kept me from winning battles against the enemy, which made me susceptible to the idea that killing myself was the only way to end my nightmare that others called life. So one more time, as an adult, I found myself heavily contemplating killing myself. This time it was with a bottle of Acetaminophen PM.

As I drifted off to sleep, I could hear the sound of my heart beating loudly and slowly. It is amongst one of the scariest sounds I had ever heard. I remember negotiating with the Lord yet feeling like His response to me was, "Daughter, there is nothing to negotiate. It's not your time, go back and live."

I rolled out of bed, crawled to the phone, and called one of my church sisters and explained what happened. She asked if I could make it to the front or back door because she was coming over with an ambulance. I did not have enough strength to get to either of them; they were both too far away. She knew the owner of the house I was renting. I assume, the owner let everyone in because the only thing I remember is the feeling of a tube being shoved down my throat. I stayed in the hospital for a few days. After my discharge, I did not leave feeling better or grateful. In fact, I felt worse. It's a bad place to be when you don't want to live, but you are too afraid to die... so, I continued to merely exist.

I thought that by relocating to California I would live a better life. Eventually my way of life became healthier. However, the early days were rough. And once again, for the last time in 2003, that old familiar spirit found me. I was seriously contemplating ending it all, plotting where and how I would do it, and wondering which one of my girls would find me and what they would feel upon finding me. However, our Father, God, loves me and my children way too much to have us endure such a burden. He always has a ram in the bush. Right in the midst of that insane, internal conversation, I received a phone call. It was a woman on the other end of the line wanting to know if I would like to meet with her to test and possibly purchase women's beauty products. I responded rudely to her by stating, "I do not have money for beauty products." The phone was silent for maybe a second, then she asked me three poignant questions:

1. Are you a Christian?
2. Do you believe in Jesus?
3. Can I pray for you?

I answered yes to all three, although the last yes was hesitant and soft. She began to pray for me unlike anyone had ever prayed for me. I could feel the absolute confidence and power in the fervent prayer, and I knew she believed deliverance was near. I immediately felt a shift as if she had a set of keys to Heaven. Neither I nor any other Christian I worshipped with prayed with such absolute authority as the woman did on the phone that day. Clearly, her foundation was built on the Solid Rock and her identity was in Jesus Christ. I cried tears I had never cried before. I muttered heartfelt, bellyaching moans and groans. It was a prayer I needed spoken over and into my life. I began to feel stronger and started praying with her. It was the absolute best prayer session I'd had to date. I did not know it then, but that woman would become my first life coach; she has been with me since that dark day in June of 2003.

After that day, I do not have major attacks from the spirit of suicide anymore, and I praise and thank God. Today, with the authority placed in me by Jesus Christ, I know who I am and whose I am. I stand in that authority. My heavenly Father has a plan and a purpose for me and I am here to fulfill His destiny for my life. I still have challenges, as we all do; however, the God in me knows it's stronger than any force that attempts to take me out.

Over the years, I learned several things about suicide as it applies to me. It is a spirit that works alone or attaches itself to other issues such as: chronic emotional, physical or mental illnesses. Since I know what it is and what it looks like, with each new experience I take strategic precautions to always guard my heart and mind. The spirit of suicide is a selfish spirit straight from the pit of hell that comes to rob, steal, kill, and destroy. I do not play with it nor do I entertain it. Neither should you.

SOUL REFLECTION:
Now that you have read my story, what do I want the takeaway to be? I want to assure the person that reads and identifies with it that you are not alone. According to the Centers for

Disease Control and Prevention, suicide takes the lives of 38,000 Americans each year. That is approximately 125 people every day, at a rate of 12 minutes per day. If you find yourself or someone you know in immediate danger, call 911 or the National Suicide Prevention Hotline at: (800) 273-8255. If your situation is not urgent or emergent but you need to talk to someone for guidance and direction, you can always reach out to me at: Admin@coachdebbiehandler.com. I pray that the protection of Psalm 91 will always be with you. God bless.

Choices that Challenged, Changes that Conquered: All in Black *and* White

KYMBERLI WILLIAMS

"My grace is sufficient for you, for my power is made perfect in weakness."

—2 Corinthians 12:9 (NIV)

I was living life with a brutally broken spirit. I felt abandoned, alone, and ashamed based on actions and treatment from my family, friends, and people of my own race. How could someone created by God in a different shade release such demonic behavior from the exact people that taught me love and belief in the Holy Spirit? What was real? Was the love of God and Christianity real? What happened to those Sunday lessons and youth worship? Where was the forgiveness? WAIT—forgiveness? What decision or choice had I made that required me to ask for forgiveness? Nothing! I fell in love with a child of God! A child of God that was a different hue than myself. That was it!

My story began in a Charleston, West Virginia. I had a great family. I had wonderful parents. Being the only child, I wanted for nothing. I grew up in a very small, rural town, and during my adolescent years I was never subjected to racism on any level. It was simply not something that was allowed in my home. My dad was a developer and owned a company that employed without discrimination. Anyone and everyone was welcome. Family, friends, and neighbors may have felt differently. It did not matter! Racism was not something that crossed the threshold of our home at any time. As a child, you do not realize the affect that one individual of a different race has on non-exposed, small minded people in all walks of life. My first memory of racism was while sitting at the dinner table during the holidays. My uncle made a black and white joke. He filled a bowl with water and tossed in salt and pepper. I do not remember the context of the joke, but I can visualize him placing his finger in the bowl and the salt and pepper splitting to opposite sides of the bowl. I was a child at that time, maybe six or seven. I remember my dad standing up from the table and stating that he would not allow such hatred in the presence of his child. He asked my uncle to leave. Again, I did not realize the significance of racism at that time, but I knew something was terribly wrong. My dad was overly protective at that point. He was preparing me to be unbiased in the real world. I was being shaped to look at all people the same, without judgment or generational ignorance. My mom and dad were dedicated Christians with very strong faith. It took my dad a little longer to accept Christ, but when he did it was a very special time for me as we were baptized together in a creek up a small hollow in the backwoods of West Virginia. As the choir stood on the side and sang "Meet Me at the River," that was the very first time I felt the significance of God's peace in my life.

The years passed, and all seemed very normal. I started junior high school and life took a huge turn. I was then exposed to classmates of a different race. Yes, I had been around African American men and women all of my life because of my father's company, but there were no children of color that attended my grade school. I was instantly in love with the different cultures, the music, the soulfulness, the commitment to God first, and strong family ties. This was not something I had experienced in my life, being an only child. I remember the very day and the very moment my heart felt something different. I was in the ninth grade, sitting in history class. There was a young man that always sat next to me in the back of the room and we joked and laughed like we had been friends since birth. This particular day, the feeling was different, and in my mind I knew this was going to be my first love. He actually called me that night! I did not think twice about the call other than the giddiness I felt over my first crush. I remember my parents asking me about the boy and I said he was a friend from school. I was apprehensive to tell my parents, not because of his race, but because this was my first dating experience. The calls continued for a while, then note passing and walks at lunch. We did not have cell phones then, so it was all handwritten exchanges. I carried a bookbag and always kept the notes inside. I loved to read them, they made me feel special. I was on my way to being the best—good grades, very active in school, and dating the star quarterback. God was in control, just like the day my dad and I were baptized. I felt free and happy!

I arrived home from school. It was a normal day. My mom always had a snack prepared; but, something was very different. A heavy feeling came over me as I walked through the door. My mom said, "Sit down and eat," in a voice that was unusual. She began to ask me questions about this "boy" and threw the notes from my bookbag on the counter, demanding answers. My parents were strict, so my immediate thought was, "I am not supposed to be dating without permission." I was wrong! It was because the guy was black. I never heard my mom talk to me the way she did that day. I was completely heartbroken, confused, and most of all wondering in my soul, where is God in all of this? The things I am hearing are nothing I had been taught, nothing I had experienced. It was exactly the opposite! I felt myself sink. I wanted to run. I wanted desperately to understand what I had done so terribly wrong simply by becoming interested in someone that had darker skin than me. This day the anchor chained itself to me. An anchor of misplaced hate and deep pain. Have you ever watched a movie where the anchor drops to the bottom of the sea and moves searching for something to anchor to; but, during the slow, methodical search for security, it creates devastating debris with no clear view for miles? That is exactly where I stood. My mind and my heart were unraveling from my personal and desperate need to understand what was real. I was anchored in my upbringing and confident in the woman I was becoming, until now. The commotion gave me pause as the clearness of how I was taught to treat everyone created in the likeness of God was now in question. All because of a boy; a boy that was funny, happy, and smart. The boy that every young girl dreams about. Except, one thing, he was not white! That evening, my parents sat me down and explained how some people would not accept me dating someone of another race. They explained that my actions may affect some family and friends and there is no going back because my image would forever be changed in their eyes. I would be known as "The little white girl that dates interracially." I would be looked at as an embarrassment. Not by the ones that birthed me, but by anyone that did not accept change. I would live a different life, one that would not come with an easy transition. I was very confused. I was happy and excited about my new guy. How could this be happening? This is not of God's teaching. My anchor was slipping and dragging through my mind as life exploded into debris.

    I returned to school the next day and told my guy the entire situation. He was not surprised. Wow, what was I missing? He said it was ok and not to worry. We just needed to be careful and keep everything a secret. I was confused, but I trusted my instincts. We were experiencing our first real love and we were determined we could handle whatever was to come. We continued to talk. The phone calls to my home became limited to times my parents were away or times I could sneak into my closet to quickly call, whispering in fear because my parents had asked that I stop all contact with him. Then it happened! People began to talk, make comments, and the hate was right in my face as my parents had predicted. I always sat near the front on the school bus, and one day as I boarded to go home, I began to hear chanting.

The entire bus erupted and chanted "N... Lover" over and over. Things were being thrown at me. I looked up to that big mirror, you know the one that the bus driver watches all of the kids through, and nothing... the bus driver did nothing. The chants continued until I exited the bus shaking, crying, and broken. Afraid to tell my parents what happened to me, I went to my room and pulled out my little Bible my mamaw had given me. I held it in my hands and asked, "Why? Please, Jesus, help me understand." That night, the nastiest, ugliest thing happened. We were awakened by burning crosses in our yard. There was no hiding the truth now. A message was being sent and me and my guy were completely exposed.

    I cannot tell you the depth of the destruction this created for my family. When I say family, I mean me, my mom, and my dad. There was really no reason to care about anyone else's feelings. My parents became more concerned for my safety. My dad started driving me to and from school, and he came to the school at lunchtime so I could sit in the car safely. The division in my school and neighborhood was evident and scary. We tried to get back to normal. I even tried attending school functions, ballgames, and dances, but the threats and taunting continued. The hate was coming from such a dark place that my parents would receive telephone calls describing what I was wearing, my whereabouts, and threats that I was not going to make it home alive. It was too much for everyone, so the decision was made that we would move from our family home. My parents purchased property in another county and the plan was to move before the next session of school. As a family, we opted for me to go to boarding school. Still hanging on to my guy in secret,

I knew it was best. Ignorance led everyone to believe that my parents shipped me off because of their own racism; but, they sent me away out of love and safety. I left, loved my school, stayed in constant contact with my guy, and visited with him on every return home. My anchor lifted for a period of time, but quickly returned after I graduated.

I returned home, and like always, I expected to return to my home church. However, although three years had passed, I was told that I could not go to the church because God would collapse the entrance on me for my behavior. I completely lost my faith. I lost the little girl inside that enjoyed those Sunday school lessons, playing the piano while my dad sang, Vacation Bible School, and reciting "The Lord's Prayer." Where are you, Jesus? I ran my mind over the Scriptures. Where in the Bible does it say not to associate with someone of another race or hue? I never learned that lesson at church or at home. I became depressed, but more so, angry. I felt betrayed by the teaching of a church I loved. I started battling internally about God's love. We are all God's children, right? I began to withdraw and ignore any idea of attending church or Christian functions. My belief in God was in question because I knew Him to be an amazing, healing, loving, kind, and forgiving, living Spirit. I was desperately in need of a renewing of faith as I left for college. I was lost. The Spirit was gone.

After leaving for college, my life did not change much. I met another man. This man was the man I knew I would marry. He was black too. I told my parents. I was determined not to hide it ever again. God filled my spirit and He placed this man in my path. God revealed Himself once again. I was a good person and my choices were of God, not of hate. My dad was my rock. He took my soon-to-be husband to the country club (with no black members) and stood in his truth. It was not looked upon well in that setting, but God was working. My dad stood up for me and he stood up for what was right. My parents were of God and non-judgmental. I got married and God blessed us with a beautiful baby boy. My son was born in January of 1991. My dad passed away at the age of 45 on Father's Day, 1991. My world collapsed. "Dear God," I asked, "Why? What have I done that again challenges my faith in this world without the very protection of my earthly father that YOU entrusted to mold me, teach me, and love me?" I became extremely bitter and unhappy. I got divorced, lost contact with my mom and struggled as a mother, a woman, and a Christian. The anchor was now whipping around in the depths of hell and I did not care.

Then, my life changed. God showed me exactly who was in charge. He had allowed the devil to drag my faith as I allowed Satan to anchor my being. I failed the test! Oh, I failed the test. But, God! God let me whip around with that anchor, too stubborn and hardhearted to understand that all I needed to do was look up and look around. My son was my answer from God. A life for a life. I simply needed to open my heart to my purpose. I asked God for forgiveness. Not for my choices, but for my selfishness, for my weakness, and for not trusting the Word and believing the teaching. He forgave me! The anchor hooked to the bottom of my soul powered its way from the depths of destruction and dysfunction within me and released itself in the name of Jesus!

In this day and time, we need to love and uplift one another. While I will never truly understand racism on any level but that which I have personally experienced, I can say this: my one and only (my son) is not black or white, he is black AND white.

SOUL REFLECTION:

There is so much more to my story, but I pray the one thing that resonates with you from me telling my truth is that there is no "or" it is always "and."

Chasing Invisible Smoke

CYNTHIA FOX EVERETT

"The Spirit of the Lord is upon Me, Because He has anointed Me To preach the gospel to the poor; He has sent Me to heal the brokenhearted, To proclaim liberty to the captives And recovery of sight to the blind, To set at liberty those who are oppressed."

—Luke 4:18 (NKJV)

I thought I had a very normal life growing up, but I guess I didn't. I thought it was normal for adults to drink alcohol, smoke cigarettes, curse each other out, and do bodily harm to each other. These things happened at cookouts, birthday parties, and other family functions, especially while playing cards on Friday and Saturday nights. It felt strange when they acted civilized. When my siblings and I would argue and fight, we would be punished. I never really understood that. I repeatedly told myself while growing up that I would never play cards or drink alcohol. I also vowed to never yell and scream at my children. None of these things meant that my grandparents and uncles didn't love me, it just meant that they had a little extra attention to give, negative or not.

My first formal introduction to mental illness was in December 2003. My baby brother was murdered on December 18, 1999. I was very angry and bitter and my relationships with my husband and my family were starting to unravel very quickly. They all acted like they were walking on eggshells and nails. It had gotten that bad. I finally decided to go to the Veteran's Hospital.

I had served in the US Army for fourteen years and spent six months, from 1990-1991, in Desert Shield/Desert Storm. I witnessed quite a few horrific things that come with war. Some things I never told anyone about. Other things had emerged from the safe place in my head even though I thought I had my memories and traumatic events (along with the mental, physical, and emotional abuse) under lock and key. Although I was in Desert Shield/Desert Storm for six months, I can only remember two months of the ordeal. It bothers me even today that I can't remember certain events. Somedays I frustrate myself trying to remember until I am in tears. At that point, I crawl into my prayer closet and pray for my Father to heal those areas of my mind and heart. I confess that it's all bigger than me and He calms my soul and spirit. I know now that me not remembering events is a way that my brain protects itself from trauma. Every now and then, when I can handle the memories, I remember certain things. I did manage to laugh a time or two while I was there, and I also made some great friendships.

When I went to the VA Hospital in 2003, I was seen by a psychiatrist and officially diagnosed with Post-Traumatic Stress Disorder (PTSD), Major Depressive Disorder, Military Sexual Trauma (MST), Anxiety Disorder, and Obsessive Compulsive Disorder (OCD). I had heard about some of these conditions, but I didn't know what they were. Most importantly I was thinking, "I know she's not talking about me." I asked the psychiatrist if she had the right file. She said yes and read my information out loud. I sat before her in great disbelief and acceptance at the same time. I'm not crazy! My family thinks I am, but I'm not. One part of me was thinking, "Finally I can get some help." The other part of me thought, "There must be two of me because I'm a black woman, a mother, a wife, and a Soldier. We don't get depressed or tired or suicidal or broken or any of the labels she is trying to pin on me."

    I quietly denied and deflected what she was saying for as long as I could. Finally, I accepted her words and asked, "What do I do from here?" She suggested a regiment of medication to start on and therapy with her at least twice monthly. I agreed quietly as fear glistened in my eyes and my body trembled softly. Yet, I walked tall and erect like a mother, a Soldier, a black woman. I walked like my mother and her mother did with their perfect imperfections. Little did I know how hard it would be to divorce myself from all of the pills that had taken over my life, my world.

    I returned home afraid to share my news in fear of being judged even more. I kept it to myself as long as I could. When I couldn't take it anymore, I screamed and yelled at everyone to just shut up! I truly knew I had to do this without my family, but I had God. I had rededicated my life to Him and I had two friends I could confide in. They were a great support system. Most importantly, I trusted them and God.

    On October 4, 2006, I was involved in a car accident and I was introduced to pain medication. Over the next two and a half years, I became addicted to them. In 2008, I buried a second brother and my life had become unbearable. In July 2008, what I thought was my final attempt at suicide was unsuccessful. On August 25, 2008, I admitted myself into a detox facility and went on to rehab. This process was about a month long. Upon leaving there, I attended numerous AA and NA meetings and eventually totally trusted God with all of my challenges in life. As I dealt with the issues I thought I had hidden and tucked away, I began to heal from the inside out. I eventually admitted myself into the mental ward at the Veteran's Hospital two more times.

I have been in therapy for the last fifteen years. The type of therapy depended on where I was mentally and what medications I was taking. I was also being counseled by my pastor. During this period, I have tried numerous psychotropic drugs that have had both positive and negative effects on my skin, my weight, my hair, my teeth, my mind (hallucinations), and my soul. It has been a long journey dealing with mental illness—the stigma, the shame, and the uncertainties from the medications. Some days, I still don't know if I'm going or coming. That's when I pray a little harder for my Father to strengthen me. He even carries me some days, and I'm fine with that as long as He never leaves me. After two years, I must change my regiment and get bloodwork done every three to four months because of the damage it can cause to my liver and kidneys. I have had some liver damage; but so far, it's under control. Some days I grow very weary dealing with mental illness and I want to quit. But, quitting isn't an option. I do get tired of taking pills, but for right now

I have to do what I have to do to see my way clearly through the smoke screen called mental illness.

I have had a lot of trial and error with mental illness. It's not a perfect science, though I wish it was. I take life and my journey with mental illness as it comes. Some days, I just don't know if I can deal with life on its terms, but I keep moving. When I can't see my way, I trust God even the more. This journey has truly strengthened my faith beyond measure. Every day that I wake up, no matter what is going on in my life, I'm just grateful to be alive. I know that "life happens" and then you live.

Mental illness affects everyone in the family, not just the person that has been diagnosed. Often, people can minimize the person and the diagnosis, unknowingly doing further damage. Mental health includes our emotional, psychological, and social well-being. It affects how we think, feel, and interact with others. Good mental health is important for every area of our lives. Many factors contribute to mental health problems. Some of the factors are biological, such as: genes or brain chemistry. Some are caused by life experiences, such as: trauma or abuse and a family history of mental health problems. People can experience diverse types of mental health problems. If you have, or believe you may have, mental health problems, it can be helpful to talk about your issues with people you trust. I trusted my pastor and a therapist I had been seeing for a while. It can be very scary to reach out for help, particularly if you don't have anyone you can trust and you are in fear of judgment. I did an excellent job of judging myself and didn't need anyone to help. I didn't need a thousand questions asked, a speech given to me on how I should have done things differently, or someone saying, "I would have been there for you" or "Get over it." People often try to tell you what you're doing wrong without totally knowing the circumstances. Finding someone to trust was the hardest part for me. I am a very private person. The guilt and shame were enough to make me want to disappear into thin air. A few times when I tried to confide in someone, I got a very long speech and a lot of misinformation.

Finding someone to trust is the second most important step. The first is admitting to yourself that you have a problem. It is all a part of the equation for healing, growth, and recovery. Mental illness comes with its own challenges and can become a part of life that often causes us to feel hopeless. We have all been tempted to quit in the face of trials. Yet, God wants us to know that He is always with us.

> "The grace of God that brings salvation has appeared to all."
> —Titus 2:11 (NKJV)

People often don't get the mental health services they need because they don't know where to start. Talk to your primary care doctor or another health professional about mental health problems. Ask them to connect you with the right mental health services. If you do not have a health professional who is able to assist you, use these resources to find help for yourself, your friends or your family members.

Resources:

- If the situation is potentially life threatening, get immediate emergency assistance by calling 911, available 24 hours a day.
- If you or someone you know is suicidal or in emotional distress, contact the National Suicide Prevention Lifeline at 1-800-273-TALK (8255). Trained crisis workers are available to talk 24 hours a day, 7 days a week. Your confidential and toll-free call goes to the nearest crisis center in the Lifeline national network. These centers provide crisis counseling and mental health referrals.
- Resources for Service Members (current and former): Military OneSource is a free service provided by the Department of Defense to service members and their families to help with a broad range of concerns, including possible mental health problems. Call and talk anytime, 24 hours a day, 7 days a week, at 1-800-342-9647.
- Resources for both Service Members and Veterans: National Resource Directory (NRD) connects wounded warriors, service members, Veterans, and their families with national, state, and local support programs. NRD is a partnership among the Departments of Defense, Labor, and Veterans Affairs.
- The Defense Centers of Excellence for Psychological Health and Traumatic Brain Injury (DCoE) provides information and resources about psychological health, post-traumatic stress disorder (PTSD), and

traumatic brain injury. To contact the center, call: 1-866-966-1020, 24 hours a day, 7 days a week or email: resources@dcoeoutreach.org.
- Department of Veterans Affairs Mental Health Resources provides information about mental health and support services specifically for Veterans. The VA Mental Health connects Veterans to mental health services the VA provides for Veterans and families.
- Vet Centers: Community-based centers that provide a range of counseling, outreach, and referral services to eligible Veterans to help them make a satisfying post-war readjustment to civilian life.
- National Center for Post-Traumatic Stress Disorder: The center's purpose is to improve the well-being and understanding of individuals who have experienced traumatic events, with a focus on American Veterans.
- DoD/VA Outreach: Moving Forward: A free, online educational and life coaching program that teaches problem-solving skills to help you handle life's challenges better. It is designed to be especially helpful for Veterans, service members, and their families.

SOUL REFLECTION:
"Whenever you find yourself doubting how far you can go; just remember how far you have come. Remember everything you have faced, all the battles you have won, and all the fears you have overcome." —Author unknown

When Morning Tarries

CHRISTINE NORMAN

"*Weeping may endure for a night, but joy cometh in the morning.*"
—Psalm 30:5b (KJV)

There is nothing like having God come through when you need Him the most—those times when your back is against the wall and there seems like there is no way out. A big comeback when we are down and out is the stuff that slogans, hashtags, and high fives are made of. We sing and shout about it, preachers preach about it: #WontHeDoIt #GodIsGood #BlessedandHighlyFavored. But what happens when midnight comes, things do not turn around, and times are so dark that it is difficult to see your way or to see or feel God. St. John of the Cross called this season the dark night of the soul and wrote a poem with the same title. In "Dark Night of the Soul," he explains that to prepare saints for a deeper union with God, this dark night comes to purify and prepare the heart.

    I remember when my own dark night started. Trouble and tragedy struck my life so hard that I often felt like I had been sucker punched. I answered the phone unsuspectingly on more than one occasion, only to hear that just when I thought things couldn't get worse, they had. I repeatedly woke up determined to have a day on top, determined not to cry, or determined to put on a happy face, only to find myself in darkness yet again. I had no idea why there were so many storms in my life and why they seemed to be lingering so long. I had experienced a radical life change when I gave my heart to God, followed by many blessings and miracles. Sure, I had problems but none that caused me to lose hope. I had a deep-rooted faith. I knew that trouble would come and though I had been enduring a rougher than normal season, I thought that I was about to come out. Little did I know that it was like waking up in the middle of the night, feeling like it was a new day, but morning was still far away.

> *"Beloved, think it not strange concerning the fiery trial which is to try you, as though some strange thing happened unto you."*
> *—1 Peter 4:12 (KJV)*

Throughout this very trying season, I trusted God, but couldn't rest. I wanted out of every uncomfortable situation. My children were hurting, my closest relationships were challenged like never before, and I was losing certainty that things would get better. One child was raped, the other robbed at gunpoint, car wrecks, church hurts, relationships ended, and that doesn't scratch the surface of all that was going on around me for a span of five years. Disappointment does not describe the depths of pain my soul experienced.

I couldn't be mad at God because I knew that I needed Him too much. Yet, there were many times that I wanted to ask, "Really, God? Did I do something wrong? I thought we were better than this!" I no longer recognized my life. I kept asking myself, "How is this my life? Where is my happy place. Where is my praise report?"

As much as I wanted to cry foul, the Scriptures reminded me that there was nothing so special about me that I should be exempted from the fiery trials that even Christ himself suffered. Though I considered myself a student of the entire Bible, somewhere along the way I forgot that God isn't caught off guard by suffering. I forgot that the Bible says it pleased the Lord to bruise Christ. I forgot that God was more interested in my calling than my comfort, and more interested in my purpose than my pleasure. I forgot that reconstruction requires demolition and breaking before any painting, landscaping, and beautification can be done. I forgot that the process is often painful. I forgot that before there could be a resurrection, there had to be a cross.

> *"Simon, Simon, Satan has asked to sift all of you as wheat. But I have prayed for you, Simon, that your faith may not fail. And when you have turned back, strengthen your brothers."*
> —Luke 22:31-32 (NIV)

Long before St. John came up with the idea of the dark night of the soul, Jesus explained such darkness to Peter. Just like with Job, Satan had asked for permission to sift Peter. Just like he had been given permission to sift Peter, I believe that Satan had been given permission to sift me. I have heard of people who say they went through difficulty and never doubted, but I was just like Peter. I don't *think* I denied him, but I am sure that there were times that my disbelief looked no different than Peter's denial. I didn't willingly or eagerly sign up to endure this sifting by Satan, but I began to learn that there were benefits to be gained from this difficult and trying process. The very act of sifting conveys the notion of removing the undesirable parts, making the initial product a better quality of substance, or sorting through to find the most valuable parts. It is often said that sometimes things must fall apart to come together, and this is precisely what sifting is all about. God does not test us for HIM to find out what we are made of—He knows that quite well. We are sifted so that we can see for ourselves. We are sifted so that we can see how much we need God and how much we need growth. Yet, we can rest assured of victory despite the shifting process because the Scriptures declare that Jesus is praying for us. Friends may sleep on us, and our hearts may be too heavy to do anything but pray for mercy and help at times, but God is praying for us.

Luke 22:32 also says that when you have turned back (or when you have recovered) strengthen your brothers. This is huge because it shows that we will come out—Jesus already declared it. He says when not if. The Scripture also shows that we have to use the strength that we gain in the struggle to strengthen others. So many are acting like they don't struggle, but for the rest of us, we need someone to share with us so that we will understand that the struggle will not kill us. People are finding themselves in despair with no hope or help. Far too many people—Christians, pastors, and leaders alike—are killing themselves or using things to cope that could ruin their lives or their families. We need to be honest and admit that struggle affects us all. If the Bible says that it rains on the just and the unjust, why do we paint the picture that we only walk in the sunshine because we have Jesus? We need to spread the word that Jesus will not exempt us from facing pain, but He will exempt us from facing pain alone. We also need to be there for others as they are going through. Luke 22:32 reminds us that it is a directive from the Lord Himself.

Night Vision

Though these dark nights that we enter can be devastating, lonely, and fearsome, they can produce in us something that the morning light can never accomplish. In them, we become keenly aware of how to walk by faith and not by sight. We stop running from pain and difficulty, and we learn how to appreciate what the dark nights are doing in us even when we don't like it. We learn how to walk in the dark. We learn that we cannot wait until daybreak to function because night could last years. We learn how to do everything in the dark—dream, create, prepare, give, love, and praise while it is dark. We adapt. We learn how the light that God has already lit inside of us is enough to sustain us even in the darkest of times. When we learn how to function in the dark, we become unstoppable. If pain and utter devastation did not kill the dreams and love inside of us, then what will? Each time we face our dark night, we are one step closer to being unafraid of the dark. Every time you go through pure hell and realize that the Lord is with you in the valley of the shadow of death, you are less afraid of the devil.

"Nothing ever goes away until it has taught us what we need to know."
—Pema Chödrön

When we resist our pain and suffering, when we hide, when we medicate, and when we deny the very existence of the pain, we prolong it. What we resist will ultimately persist. What we mask only hides from the one wearing the mask—it is often evident to those close to us. Running from our pain prolongs it because the very purpose of this pain in our lives is to teach us what needs to be healed and what needs our attention, and to prepare us for what is ahead. God loves us far too much to allow us to remain the same. And because the good times often intoxicate us and lull us to sleep, wake up calls are often necessary to gain our attention. Through my pain, I have learned some invaluable lessons, and because of that, I no longer regret the things that I have been called to face.

Lessons from the Dark:
1. Pray without ceasing.
   God hears even when it seems He has stopped listening.

2. Pain and suffering are inevitable and will only stop me if I let them.
Setbacks and stumbling blocks can only stop us if we allow them to. However, if we use pain and suffering just like bodybuilders use heavy weights, we can use difficulty as the fitness room of our lives. Pain is often required either by my Creator or my current circumstances. It serves me better to ask what I can do with what I face instead of why me?
3. Do not label things good or bad but rather focus on what is necessary or unnecessary. If I adjust my perspective about what good and bad really are, some things that I dreaded become much smaller and some of the things that I chased so desperately loosen the grip they once had on my life.
4. Whatever I have right now is what I need right now. I have no lack and I am not overwhelmed.
If there is nothing that I can do, I give it to God; if there is something that I can do, I do it. If there is something that I struggle with doing, I enlist the help of God and trusted others. If there is no one to help, I do not assume that I am helpless; instead, I assume that God wants me to face it alone and will strengthen me to do what is at hand. There is tremendous power that comes from believing that everything is EXACTLY as it should be. If help is needed, help will show up. If resources are needed, resources will show up. I have learned to play the hand that I have. Perhaps God wants me to see

how much I can do when all I have are Him, me, and all that He has placed in me.

5. Though I must go it alone at times, I still need others.

Independence is not isolation. I need other people, and I must always caution against building walls to keep people out. Doing so may isolate me from hurt, but it also keeps the good in me from reaching others and the good in others from reaching me. Instead, I must forgive those who have hurt me, free myself from bitterness and the fear of rejection, and build a tribe of a safe and healthy network of people. In this network, we all grow from the iron sharpening iron that God intended we have in community.

6. Nothing replaces human care and concern in anyone's life.

God intended that our need for human care be met through Him, and the vehicle that He so often uses is human relationship. We must never make the mistake of thinking that anyone is "too" anything that we do not need human care and concern. The rich need it no less than the poor. Those extremely smart and talented need it no less than those with average intelligence. Those who are strong in anything, leading anything, abundant anywhere, just may need it more because everyone assumes that they can go without it. Many brush off "the strong," minimizing their struggles. I know because I have faced this. This is dangerous, far from the truth, and could be why people that seem to "have it all" end

up in very fragile places. Those of us labeled strong are not superhuman, we just have decided to keep going no matter how hard life gets. Sometimes we don't even realize that we are running hard with tanks that are critically low until something breaks down. Nothing exempts any person from darkness, and a broken heart feels the same in the palace and the poorhouse.
7. Mental health matters just as much as physical health.

If you would not do self-care on a broken bone or internal organ, do not do the same with your mind, heart, and soul. Inner care is as crucial as outer care. Poor mental health is said to be at the root of many diseases. I do not advocate for mental health just because I am studying it, I am studying it because I realized its importance and I want to spread awareness. Some of our suffering comes from things we need to learn to do better and we need a second set of professional eyes.

SOUL REFLECTION:

> "But he knows the way that I take; when he has tried me, I shall come out as gold."
> —Job 23:10 (ESV)

My dark night spanned over five years and the underlying issues were brewing for much longer. I have learned how to thrive in the dark. I have learned to enjoy the joyful moments as they come. I work hard at staying present in today without ruining the present with the pain of yesterday or the worry of tomorrow. I rejoice that despite my fears and doubts, I still have faith and I know that God is indeed keeping me when I am weak. Faith is not evidenced by the fact that you never doubt—for even John the Baptist asked Jesus, "Are you the one or should we look for another?" Faith is evidenced by the fact that we never stop believing once and for all. When we keep coming back to God after we have been knocked down by the trials of life, we can say like Job, "Though He slays me, yet will I trust Him." Morning may tarry, but it indeed comes. And when it does, after a season of growth through struggle, it finds us so much better than before.

The Cycle of Generational Dysfunction

KIMBERLY SOLOMON

"I call heaven and earth as witnesses against you today, that I have set before you life and death, the blessing and the curse; therefore, you shall choose life in order that you may live, you and your descendants."

—Deuteronomy 30:19 (AMP)

Can you imagine a mother not wanting her daughter? Can you imagine a woman forced to choose between her pregnancy and her drugs? Can you imagine the pain a mother must feel knowing that her vision of a fairy tale is falling apart right before her eyes? I want you to imagine that pain and then multiply it by two. Better yet, multiply it by three generations. That is just a piece of my story and why, for so many years, I had to talk to my soul! I had to encourage myself daily. Over and over I would ask the question, "Why didn't my mom get help?" When people were trying to figure out their "why" in life, I was busy trying to figure out the "why" in my mother's life.

It took me a long time to figure out that I couldn't apologize for my mother's behavior. I couldn't make up for the mistakes that my mother made. How many of us pass on tradition after tradition and never take the time to realize how damaging or detrimental it can be? We pass on traditions and cycles from one generation to the next.

The year was 1980 when my mother got pregnant. She was living in New York when she met my father. They began to date, and my mom found out that she was pregnant. She told my grandmother that she was pregnant and my grandmother told her to "Get married or go to hell and burn!" I believe on that day all that she took from the conversation with her mother was that one statement. Since my mother held onto her mothers' words, she immediately approached my father about marriage. My father loved my mother, so they got married. The same love that brought them together was the same love that tore them apart.

When I was two, my parents divorced. My father loved that my mother was from up north and that she was different from the other women that he dated. Yet, when his career was taking off and he began to run for office and get groomed for politics, he felt like the "round-the-way" girl wasn't good for his image. He wanted someone that was more versed in politics and comfortable mingling with the upper class, or so he thought. He didn't think my mom would perform well in that environment and over time she began to confirm his thoughts. She just didn't want to be that person. Half of her wanted to be the trophy wife and the other half wanted to be independent. We found out later that she was literally torn in half mentally by that decision.

From the age of two to twelve, I began to raise myself. My mother was on her second child with no husband in sight. My older brother's father had already dumped her and now my father was out of the picture. She began to cling to my brother as if that was her husband. She began to establish a dysfunctional relationship that would draw a wedge between us for years to come. I didn't realize it until years later, but I was simply looking for someone that would love me and validate me as a treasure. My father was in and out of my life during those years, trying to make it big as a stockbroker.

At the age of twelve, my virginity was taken from me by a boy that was four years older than me. Since my mother didn't have time for me, she didn't notice when I was gone. I would often come home and she would brag about the time she spent at church helping other children, share their wonderful testimonies, then disappear again. Her body was with me, but her mind was far away. I found out later in life that she would burn me with cigars out of spite for my father. She knew that he loved cigars and that he loved me, so something inside of her told her to take the pain out on me. She had hoped to gain a husband, but in return she gained a child that she had to raise on her own.

From age twelve to seventeen, I lived my life the best way I could. I would talk to myself and write poetry to keep myself encouraged. I would even have fake talk shows in the bathroom to pretend that I was interviewing my better self. I was interviewing the grown-up Kimberly that had made something of herself and was someone that I could be proud of. I began to spend more time in my dreams than in my reality. My dreams provided me the opportunity to escape from a world that was so unpleasant. A world that I thought had forgotten about me. I kept hearing my mom talk about her God, but I didn't know Him for myself.

The first opportunity that I got to be on my own, I took it. I graduated from high school at the age of seventeen and I decided to get a job. I looked in the classifieds and saw an ad for a dancer. I wasn't sure what kind of dancer, so I called my friend and asked her to go with me to the interview. When the location of the interview was a bar named Brass Monkey, I should've known better. When we entered the dimly lit bar, an old Caucasian man came from behind the door. He quickly ushered us to the bar to fill out paperwork. I didn't even take time to read the paperwork; I heard dollar signs and began to sign my name. Little did I know my life was about to take a huge turn.

For the next six months I worked at this bar and made a lot of money. They decided to let me only work when special guests came to the bar. One night, a very familiar rap artist came into the bar and they called me to work. He offered me a job to tour with him. I went to our home and told my mother about the job offer. She forced me to understand that God wouldn't be pleased with me if I went to do that. For once in my life, I listened to what she was saying, and it made sense. I was able to hear about a God that I didn't know. She took the time to stop and talk to me and help me understand this God that she had served for so many years. She began to talk to my soul. She told me of a God that loved me. She confessed that she didn't want me in the beginning and that she was trying to kill what God sent to heal her.

That message changed my life. I stopped working at the Brass Monkey. I sat in the living room that day and began to cry out to God. I didn't know how to approach Him, but I let my spirit cry out for me. As I laid out in the Lord's presence,

He began to speak to me. He began to show me that I was His child and that He loved me. He loved me in spite of my faults and my issues. He showed me how He created me to worship Him in spirit and in truth. He showed me how to praise dance in the spirit and that when I danced in the bar it was perverting what He created me to do. When I awoke, I was in the middle of the living room in a puddle of my own tears. My eyes were bloodshot and my hands and legs began to move. I could hear music in my head. I got my mother's attention from the other room and told her that I needed to dance. That was my first praise dance. Right in the middle of my mother's living room! I didn't understand that this wasn't the end of my life; this was merely the beginning of a new life to come.

I decided that I needed a change; so, I called the Air Force recruiter and decided to take him up on his offer. When I was in high school they tried to recruit me, but I didn't want to go. Now I knew that after all I had been through, if I got away from my current situation I would have a better chance of being successful. Little did I know that the issue wasn't my location, the issue was my soul. I had to talk to my soul! My soul was under attack!

Let me explain the meaning of my soul being under attack. We are made up of three parts—spirit, soul, and body. Hebrews 4:12 (ESV) tell us, "For the word of God is living and active, sharper than any two-edged sword, piercing to **the division of soul and of spirit**, of joints and of marrow, discerning the thoughts and intentions of the heart."

We see in this passage of Scripture that the soul and spirit can be divided and that it is the Word of God that pierces our heart to bring the division of soul and spirit, something that only God can do.

As human beings, we live eternally as a spirit, we have a soul, and we dwell in a body.

Our body is the entire material or physical structure of a human being; it is the physical part of a person. Our soul consists of the mind, the will and the emotions.

The greatest form of warfare is in your mind! My mom has suffered from three nervous breakdowns and we took care of her for four years. The enemy told me every day that I would lose my mind just like her. I had to rebuke that voice and talk to my soul!

You see, the only reason I'm still here is because when my soul was under attack, I let go and let God be God! Even when I read the Word, it didn't stop the enemy from messing with me. I used to cry myself to sleep and ask God why these things happened to me. I even tried to take my own life because I believed that my mom loved my brother more than me and I would be doing her a favor if I left. But God showed me that He never left me. Because evil is in the world evil things will happen, but that doesn't mean He doesn't love me. His job is to judge, my job is to love. God showed me that I needed to talk to myself and love myself! Love who He created me to be!

Over the years to come I would continue to live a life that wasn't pleasing to God but was pleasing to myself. I made a baby with a man that I hardly knew, and when I called my mom for advice she told me the same thing that her mother told her. So rather than burning in hell, I got married, only to find out years later that he wasn't even the father of the baby and now I was at a crossroads. I was embarrassed and ashamed all at the same time. I began to talk to my soul! I turned back to God, as there was nowhere else to go.

That was in 2002. By 2007, I thought I had learned my lesson. I was living in Alabama and I was leading the praise dance team for a megachurch. Life was good. I was very active in church and practicing celibacy. But, on a cold night in February, I was faced with the same dilemma I had been faced with before. It was Valentine's Day and I felt depression come over me because I didn't have a Valentine and my father wasn't in my life. I began to relive the pain of being a fatherless child. I received a phone call from a friend and once again the door was opened. He came over to comfort me, or so I thought. We had sex that night, and three months later I found out I was pregnant. Once again, I was faced with shame and embarrassment. The leader of the dance team was pregnant! How could this happen?! I knew immediately what I was going to do. I wasn't going to call my mom, I was going to get an abortion. I wanted to kill what God was sending to heal!

I called the abortion clinic and made an appointment. As the receptionist scheduled my appointment, I could hear the faint screams of young girls in the back room. I tried to ignore them, but I couldn't. When I got to the clinic, I filled out my paperwork hoping that the guilty feeling would go away. I sat in the cold waiting room all alone. I stared at the dull blue paint on the wall. I glanced at the paint chipping on the chairs and the counters. I tried not to notice the floor with random blood stains blending into the tile. Before I could walk out of the door without being noticed, the receptionist called my name. I looked around and when I didn't move the nurse came over to me. I heard her same my name, but I was still paralyzed. I felt her grab my arm and lift me up out of the chair. As I began to walk with her, I heard a loud screech come from another room! I was no longer paralyzed. I grabbed my purse, ran out of the front door and never looked back. I sat in my car and cried for hours. I remember hearing God in a still small voice. He said, "'Call to Me and I will answer you, and I will tell you great and mighty things, which you do not know.'" I now know that it was Jeremiah 33:3 (NASB).

I did not abort my daughter that day and I didn't abort what God was trying to heal in me. In 2007, after I gave birth to my daughter, the doctor told me that I was diagnosed with cervical cancer. He told me that I needed surgery. I got the surgery and decided to give my life totally to Christ. The doctor also told me that I would live but that I would never have any more children. I was tired of living the way that I was living, so that was all the confirmation I needed. In 2012, I was found by my God-mate and my life was forever changed. We met at church on the intercessory team and became good friends. Five months into the friendship, God told us to get married and we've been together ever since. He had three children, I had two children and we made three more children despite what the doctor said. We talked to our souls!

SOUL REFLECTION:
I want to encourage you to break the cycle despite your upbringing, circumstances and shortcomings. Break the cycle! This is what I say to my soul and it frees me: "I am not my mother. I am healed, and I am whole! The giants I don't fight, my children will have to fight! I'm a giant slayer!" THE CYCLE OF DYSFUNCTION IS BROKEN!

My Brokenness: His Undying Love!

SHARON L. GRAVES

"I am the LORD that healeth thee."
—Exodus 15:26 (KJV)

Today, I am a woman of faith who knows that God created me with and for a soul purpose. I am humbled and eternally grateful to Him for not having forgotten me.

My life had been comprised of many broken pieces. Today I understand that those pieces were a reflection of the brokenness of my internal state of being. Through my brokenness and reckless intensions to make bad choices, the unimaginable happened to me—I collided into this undying love. "For I am persuaded that neither death nor life, nor angels nor principalities nor powers, nor things present nor things to come, nor height nor depth, nor any other created thing, shall be able to separate us from the love of God which is in Christ Jesus our Lord."—Romans 8:38, 39 (NKJV)

After five years of prison; three plus years of homelessness; eight years of drug and alcohol abuse; what seemed like a lifetime of people addiction; seven years of physical, mental, and sexual abuse; ten years of emotional abuse;

oppression; depression; low self-esteem; suicidal tendencies; issues of abandonment; an unquenchable thirst for belonging, acceptance, and "love;" void of identity; and broken and crushed in heart and spirit, I was awakened.

When He pulled me out of the wreckage, there was insurmountable damage and resuscitation (which would be nothing short of a miracle) was my only means of survival. But, a voice in my head had become my convincing "friend" who often reminded me that I was a failure, the world and my children would be better off without me, my mother never loved me, and that just as I had been a disappointment to my children, I too was her greatest disappointment. I had succumbed to the voice of this friend. You know, the one that was always there when no one else was, the one I could count on. It wasn't going anywhere, and it was my only true friend. At least that's what it convinced me to believe.

I had taken a bad fall, and this time it was right. I didn't want to get up. I was tired, broken, empty, crushed, and I was ashamed. I had arrived at an internal place of nothingness, convinced of what the voice had been telling me: "You will never be nothing, you will never fit in, you will never belong, you will never be accepted, you will never be pretty. Better yet, you will never be." Why did God create me? What was my purpose? I was on a constant quest in my heart and mind to get the answers to those questions, but they always seemed to elude me. The internal emptiness of not belonging or being accepted was the dark cloud that seemed to forever haunt me.

> "My substance was not hid from thee, when I was made in secret, and curiously wrought in the lowest parts of the earth. Thine eyes did see my substance, yet being unperfect; and in thy book all my members were written, which in continuance were fashioned, when as yet there was none of them."
>
> —Psalm 139:15-16 (KJV)

It was as if someone had taken or hidden my place in life and I stumbled aimlessly around in the dark trying to find it. I kept getting lured in, knocked down, diminished, and shamed only to come up empty-handed, depleted, and void of self, hope, and love. I was void of the very essence of my being. If only I knew what that was.

I didn't wake up one day and order this life, but my choices served it up. And the price I had to pay was to drink this bitter cup publicly. My brokenness was laid out as a public funeral with an open casket and each passing day the people got my life to view, some with sadness others with disgust; but, none sadder or more disgusted than me.

> "If you see one overtaken in a fault, ye which are spiritual, restore such a one in the spirit of meekness; considering thyself, lest thou also be tempted."
>
> —Galatians 6:1 (paraphrased)

I was lost in addiction and no one could see that this fault had overtaken me. Now I understand why none of them could or would rescue me. I was as the walking dead, an empty shell filled with darkness and turmoil with the chains and shackles of addiction, shame, and low self-esteem taunting and dragging me to the block of slavery. I was naked and ashamed for all to see and to look upon my filth, my disgust, my shame, my low self-esteem, my self-hate, my mishaps, my mistakes, and all my open wounds.

My scars and lashes each had their own voice and story to reveal. And as I was looked down upon, snared at, tried, judged, and condemned, my shame plummeted me to a place of internal darkness and brokenness where I peeped out at others who were peeping back at me while pointing, staring, laughing, judging, and condemning me. I felt that maybe they had that right and I deserved every charge and assumption.

To this day, I can vividly recall the signs that I ignored. And that night that I allowed or maybe even convinced Phil to stick me with that needle, was the night I consciously died. I became disconnected and thought it was the euphoria of the moment that enveloped me. All the noise had stopped, and I was free from the stresses of life as well as the responsibilities that should have mattered to me. But, I didn't understand that it would be that false sense of freedom that would immediately elude me and the chase would be empty and cost me everything—my principles, morals, values, integrity, dignity, self-respect, the respect of others and my family, loved ones and friends, and if possible my soul. My addiction was taking my life and it was quickly gaining ground for public view.

I died in a moment of euphoria to a place of false security. When I returned to reality, I watched our lives (mine and my children) slip through my fingers. I lost my sense of loyalty and commitment to myself and my family. And the very hands that once provided nurture, security, and love were now the ones helplessly and hopelessly chained and shackled in addiction. A heart once filled with the hope of future possibilities and aspirations was now skeptical and entangled in a web of brokenness, sadness, and shame due to unhealthy choices.

> *"For what shall it profit a person, if they should gain the whole world, and lose their own soul?"*
> —Mark 8:36 (paraphrased)

There was a constant battle to vanish while remaining, to die while merely existing, to dwell in the dark for loss of the light, to drown in sorrow while journeying through memories of laughter, to lie in the cold in search of the warmth, to keep waking up and crying sometimes profusely because God didn't honor my wish to literally lay me down to eternal sleep. I was tired of fighting, looking for, hoping for, and praying for that end, which for me was a resting place because I no longer knew how or desired to live.

"Pass me not, O gentle Savior, Hear my humble (desperate, twisted, mangled) cry; While on others Thou art calling, Do not pass me by."

I often wondered had I disappointed God too that not even He wanted anything to do with me dead or alive? That even He was ashamed of me? That even He wanted to punish me, look upon my shame, condemn me, and make me pay for my mistakes, my foolery, my folly? Who am I and what kind of person must I be that not even the love of God or His mercy would be graced upon me?

I can recall that at about the age of eight or so, all of the other children at a revival were being saved by God except for me. Like me, they were crying; then suddenly, one by one, they were jumping up and down with excitement exclaiming, "Thank you, Jesus. Thank you, Jesus. Thank you!" I felt absolutely nothing but ashamed that God didn't pick me. And as I pondered this during that Sunday morning service following the revival, while alone on the back pew as the baptism was about to take place, I wondered through tears in my eyes and another crack in my heart what was wrong with me that Jesus didn't save me? Then I heard a voice clearly say, "Because God doesn't love you. You don't belong to God." That voice, the hurt, and the feelings of doom haunted me and impacted the trajectory of my thinking and my life far into adulthood.

And after all my shortcomings, mishaps, and mess-ups, while behind prison walls, by no means could I have ever imagined that there would or could be a sovereign plan for me.

And then God spoke and said...

"For I know the thoughts that I think toward you, saith the LORD, thoughts of peace, and not of evil, to give you an expected end."

—Jeremiah 29:11 (KJV)

I spent what seemed like a lifetime in self-sufficiency searching and yearning for "love," only to be awakened and surrender to the truth that love was there all the while—patiently, kindly, and lovingly waiting. And love, in the very essence of God, was watching over me.

His love carried me, covered me, protected me, and kept me, not only from the dangers of the world but even from the danger of myself. Whenever I look back over my life and recall the times that I was angry with God, accused God, and even felt hatred toward God, it was Him that carried me over and over and over again through dark places, unhealthy decisions, bad choices, and detrimental circumstances. For I had long given out and given up on hope, desire, and attempts to live; yet, God came where I was and rescued me. When I allowed myself to be convinced that I was left to come through and make it on my own, it was then that God "carried" me.

"Greater love hath no man than this, that a man lay down his life for his friends."

—John15:13 (KJV)

God loved me all the while. And not only did He love me, but He considered and called me friend.

Belonging was of utmost importance to me. I gave myself and my identity away in search of it. But, God extended it to me freely. He paid the ultimate price that I may have and know His undying love for me. And today, I am eternally grateful! When God found me, I was at the threshold of death and my only wish was to die because I no longer knew how to live; my life had become one big, black, empty hole and I had sunk more than six feet under. But, God came where I was and rescued me from death. He charged me to live and not die. He saved me from myself and reckless intentions to make bad choices.

Just when I was convinced that there was no need to live and that God didn't care, He showed up, proved me and the destroyer wrong, and loved me out of hell and torment. Alleluia and glory to God forever! He taught me how to love myself, how to be good to myself, and how to blossom in grace and humility. I am so glad that God's love for me was far greater than my wish to die. Now, because of Him and His love for me, I am awake.

I am awake to love and purpose, the healthy and raw emotions of pain and fear, the essence of my being, the worth of my tears, every breath that I breathe, and the pulsating of every heartbeat. I am awake to life and all it has to give.

I am awake to a journey holding wonders treasures, temptations, challenges, delicacies, and fears all to teach, stretch, grow, mature, and bridle me. This journey will strengthen my depth of knowledge into the fundamentals of life, understanding of my personal strengths and weaknesses, personhood, and well-being. And if properly received and applied, it will assist me in becoming the me I am meant to be.

I am awake to my mistakes and the ability to be free. I am awake to my differences and my need to fit in. I am awake to embracing the simplicities and complexities of all that I am! I am awake to the ins and outs of love—the laughter, romance, pain, the unwarranted games and gains, and the expense thereof.

I am awake to the understanding and acceptance that love sometimes encompasses a depth, height, and width that can for some be unattainable and for others unexplainable.

Love blossoms in rays of gentleness, patience, long suffering, peace, hope, grace, compassion, support, and much more. The "still waters" of love runs deep, is rich in many pleasures, and evolves into bonds everlasting.

I am awake to dreams and visions that dance in my head. I am awake to walk in the confidence that I am enough and that I have a new life to live, a new hope to give, a friendship to offer, and a lifeline to extend life, hope, and love to another. I am awake to the truth that I am not a victim but a victor, and I choose to live and walk victoriously in this life God has granted me!

I am awake to the revelation that we all have a purpose in life from the very day that we are born, but we are not all awakened to that revelation in the instance of that birth. Therefore, to be awakened to one's God-given purpose is not predicated on being born. Until revelation awakens this truth, a life cannot be fully lived, but merely existing in the shadows and darkness of insecurities, uncertainties, feelings of fear and abandonment, and issues of rejection (whether real or imagined) until it is awakened. For many, purpose has been revealed through sorrow, pain, and rejection.

SOUL REFLECTION:

As I reflect on my life, abuse didn't physically kill me; yet, I died a package of "damaged goods" from being kicked, punched, and thrown around. Dismissed was the sign: "Fragile, handle with care." The absence of a hug, smile, and nurturing wasn't intended for my demise; yet, I died from fear, darkness, emptiness, and a thirst to be held, liked, accepted, and loved, not only by others but also by myself. Now I stand unapologetically awakened in His undying love and grace with soul-purpose, gratefulness, peace, joy, and self-love.

Abandoned, Molested, and Abused Before My Awakening

SHEILA MALLOY-HALL

For I will restore health to you, and your wounds I will heal, declares the LORD, because they have called you an outcast:...."
—Jeremiah 30:17 (ESV)

The year was 2013—one of my most difficult years to date. What I remember most is how despondent and lonely I truly was. On the outside, I appeared happy. I had become a master at disguising my truth. In fact, doing so became my norm. For most of my life, I never operated from a place of wholeness; but, I didn't recognize it. Instead, I lived in a constant state of survival, all the while lacking a connection to my true identity. For years, I operated in my norm: getting up each morning, dressing, going to work and ensuring that no one knew I had just spent the previous evening with my covers overhead, submerged in my tears. On the inside, I was downhearted, downtrodden, and in a state of despair.

As 2013 was coming to an end, so was I. My life had become more than I could bear. I no longer had the strength to fight the lie I had been living. For me, I likened my life to a game of double-dutch—bouncing back and forth, waiting for the right time to jump in. Often feeling anxious, I wondered if I really had the strength to pursue the life I'd frequently dreamt of or would I make a fool of myself in that pursuit? It seemed pretty clear to me that my time on this earth had come to its unnatural end. My days were dark and lonely. As 2014 approached, I knew I couldn't spend any more of my days suffering with the overwhelming aches in my belly. My desire to be accepted and loved was simply too engulfing. The secrets. The lies. The abuse. All of the unanswered "Whys?" had won the battle.

I cried out to my God. Wait. Why could I no longer hear His voice? I screamed out to Him and all I heard were the echoes of my screams. Okay. That did it. I finally threw in the towel. My life was worthless. Why continue living with the weight of the anguish?

So, there I was, alone and preparing to do the unthinkable.

Travel back in time with me as I share with you what led up to the unthinkable.

Although I did pretty well at double dutching my way through life, I didn't do as well at showing up and being comfortable with the woman who stared back at me in the mirror. The woman in the mirror was always looking past me—as if I were transparent—constantly reminding me of my painful past and how I would never be able to go on living my life without her.

Abandoned

I was born in 1966. It's funny how people get so excited about their birthdays. Now, I'm not saying I don't get excited about mine because I do; however, the day I was born, I can't say there was anything special about the moment. The problem is I don't know anything about my birth. Most people share the story of their birth as it was told to them, but I am not that girl. I cannot tell you my birth story. What I can tell you is what happened a couple of days after my birth... as it was told to me.

I have no idea about the specificities of the event, but I do know my mother left me at the hospital. From what I was told, my grandmother was who brought me home from the hospital. I don't really recall having a clear concept that my grandmother wasn't my mother until the age of twelve. My birth mother was around, but I never went home with her. At the age of 12, I started gaining more insight into who my mother truly was.

You see, all I ever heard about my birth was that my mother checked herself out of the hospital and left me behind. I recall a time when my mother was standing on my grandmother's front porch crying and asking, "Let me take my daughter home, Mama." My grandmother replied "No" while reminding my mother that she left me behind and obviously didn't want me.

Years later, there I sat in a room with my mother, my grandmother, and two strangers. I remember there being lots of crying and hearing the name of my biological father for the first time. I also remember the adults in the room talking about me as if I wasn't even there, and I recall feeling scared and confused. At the end of the session, the decision was made that the woman in the room, whom I didn't know, was going to take me home with her. I lived with that woman and her children for some time. She worked for Social Services and helped troubled families. My time with her turned out to be an excellent experience. Eventually, I returned to my grandmother's home, but not without spending time with my mother and siblings on the weekends. When I visited my mother's home, I didn't find comfort there. In the confines of her home, I experienced some traumatic things that would lend themselves to the secrets I held close to me... the secrets that gave life to my state of brokenness.

Molestation

I grew up surrounded by strong women who had very dominating personalities. While the women were very strong, I believe there was a great deal of pain in their lives. They tried their best to hide that pain. I wonder if they hid it because of embarrassment or if they were raised to understand: "You don't tell your family's business."

I believe those generational behaviors were instilled in me. I, too, was a strong woman. I, too, was hiding my pain. I was always looking for something while having no idea about the very thing I sought after. Confusion. I know. I knew I wanted more for myself than the load of pain I carried and kept hidden. I carried the pain of some awful experiences from my past. And I have no doubt the pain I bore was the same as the women in my family. They possessed a strength that was meant to protect them and enabled them to mask their brokenness. Just as I did, the women in my family longed for love, protection, acceptance, and freedom from the chains that held them captive.

As a young girl, I was molested. I kept the dirty, little secret hidden deep down inside. I knew I wasn't the only female in my family who was violated by the men in the family, but, they too kept it to themselves. As for me, I was distressed for years. I dressed up that pain and moved forward with my life. I believe this to be true for the other women in my family who were sexually violated as well.

Dear Women in my family,

I am the voice of our past, present, and future.
I will no longer be silent because I love all of you.

"The LORD is close to the brokenhearted and
saves those who are crushed in spirit."

—Psalm 34:18 (NIV)

Domestic Violence

Domestic violence and abuse can happen to anyone at any time, including me. I didn't immediately recognize my situation as abuse. At the time that I was going through, domestic violence wasn't talked about openly as it is today. The help simply wasn't there for victims. I did call 911 once or twice, but when the police arrived it was as if they became therapists. They would say things like, "Ma'am, you all can work it out." I can't fail to mention that in the presence of the law, my ex performed as if he was filled with great remorse for his actions, further encouraging the ideology that we could, indeed, work it out. At the time my now ex-husband and I met, I was already isolated from my family. I wanted so badly to be loved, I didn't immediately identify the abuse when it reared its ugly head. I ignored his mean side and excused it away with, "Oh, it will pass." I often thought he was homesick, especially since he left his family behind in another country to relocate to the states. Because of that, I found myself tolerating his abuse and making excuses for his behavior. Again, I silenced my truth.

The abuse started subtly with accusations and intimidation. Eventually, the threats became physical. The beatings were awful, sometimes resulting in injuries that would send me to the hospital. I suffered in silence. I will admit that there were times I was hopeful things would change, so I stayed in the relationship. Meanwhile, I was isolated from family and friends, psychologically threatened, and beaten down physically. I couldn't find the energy to work up a plan to leave my situation.

NOTE THE TYPES OF ABUSE:
Physical, Sexual, Verbal, Psychological, and Financial

Now that you are aware of the pains of my past, let me return to that dark place for a moment. I promise to bring you back safely.

On that dreadful day near the end of 2013, I exhaled, cried, and finally made the commitment to act on a thought that haunted me for most of my life: suicide. I decided the easiest way to end my life would be to hang myself. As I stood on a chair with an extension cord around my neck, I began to think about my life: abandoned as an infant, molested as a toddler and teen, and severely abused during my first marriage. There was no way I could continue living such an unhappy life.

I struggled with getting the extension cord into the vent. After trying for a while, I was both unsuccessful and exhausted. I removed the cord from around my neck, climbed down off the chair and fell to my knees, crying uncontrollably and asking God to help me. I heard God clearly say, "You shall live." The next couple of hours after that are a blur. In the moment, I knew I was experiencing something completely foreign. At the same time, I no longer felt alone. It was time for me to release the pains that had manifested in other areas of my life due to the deep, dark secrets I kept hidden within my soul. The time for healing came as I acknowledged that God was calling me to my next chapter—one where I would experience a closer walk with Him and a freedom I could never imagine.

As daylight began to shine through the windows, I rose from the fetal position I had balled myself up into and stood tall. I basked in the experience of being with God and recalled His promise to me and my promise to Him. I promised that I would share my story with those He assigns me to. In that moment, it was revealed to me that my past was still showing up in my present. My life had been filled with trauma and fear. Through my awakening and with God's grace, I wanted to live! I wanted to live a different kind of life, begin my healing journey, and be free of the mental and physical abuse of my past. With determination, courage, faith, and professional support, my personal Healing 2 Grace journey began. Today, my journey continues; however, I use the lessons I learned to inform, inspire, and encourage others to choose a life that is free from abuse and domestic violence. I desire to embolden others to be filled with health, joy, purpose, and empowerment.

Healing 2 Grace: I'm Winning!

After all I had experienced in my life, God actually had a plan for ME! During my encounter with God, Healing 2 Grace was birthed. Healing 2 Grace is an organization that addresses the impact and aftermath of abuse and domestic violence on professional women through counseling, social support services, training, and technical assistance. The mission of Healing 2 Grace is to end the shame and stigma attached to survivors who have experienced abuse and domestic violence. We work to change the narrative from "Why did they stay?" to "They left, are now healed, and became empowered!"

I understood that God wanted me to share my story, but I didn't know where to begin. Still, I didn't question His plan and was attentive to His guidance. God's grace will always cover me as I move forward with my healing. My mess happened so that my message would help others. There are many women like me—broken, lacking internal fulfillment, and at war with their disguise to the point that their external success gives the appearance that they have it all together. I'm all too familiar with living life in bondage, feeling as if I'm gasping for air every minute of every day.

As I began my healing journey, which included seeing a therapist and spending quality time with God, the release from telling my story was huge. There was an astounding relief in saying I was abused and molested as a young girl. There was an astonishing relief in saying that as a woman, I was beaten and left for dead at the hands of an abusive mate. Speaking my truth has been so freeing! I understand that my worth is priceless. Now, I own my unadulterated truth and understand just how powerful it is. I have spent most of my life trying to please people, seeking their acceptance and love. Today, I am working to please only God.

I want other women to know they are not alone, their past pains do not define them, and GOD has a plan and purpose for their pain. I once felt stuck, struggled with trust, and was very defensive. Today, I no longer allow what happened to me in the past to dictate my future.

My advice to you is:
1. Spend time with God.
2. Confront your past.
3. Ask for help.
4. Forgive yourself.
5. Get to know yourself.
6. Everyday self-care is necessary. Do something just for you.

SOUL REFLECTION:
There is beautiful strength in each of us. But, I didn't always recognize my strength or see my beauty. Through my healing, I acknowledge my beauty and celebrate my strength. I am strong and walking boldly in my healing. I am fully awakened in my life. Healing is my birthright!

Healing is beautiful, and your life is waiting for you to fully awaken and walk in your strength because it's your birthright.

The Unthinkable That Happened

LAQUITA HOGAN

"For I consider that the sufferings of this present time are not worthy to be compared with the glory which shall be revealed in us."
—Romans 8:18 (NKJV)

The ole saying "Life happens," hit closer to home than ever before. I asked God, "Is this really happening to me right now?!" I'm a week away from getting married to my soul mate, and my mom is not able to attend. Feelings of disappointment and anger began to fill my thoughts. No amount of comfort or phone calls helped. I just needed my mom to see me as the beautiful bride she knew I would be.

Unlike any other conversation with my grandma, she brought up how my mom had been in so much pain for a week and was barely mobile. I thought to myself, "This sounds like pain from drinking too much soda." So, I didn't feel a concern that it could be serious; my focus was on completing the final details of my wedding. My grandma, who I see as the Queen of Remedies, would find her something to take and this would all clear up in a few days. The next day, I left work as normal and headed straight home to relax with my fiancé and two daughters. I decided to call and check on my mom. The conversation was really short and she could barely complete her sentences, let alone sit up according to my grandma. Immediately I heard the voice of God say, "Take her to the hospital." I thought to myself, "She will be fine. We never go to the hospital for anything unusual." The distance between where her and I lived also played a part in me wanting to let a few more days go by, just to see if she would feel better. But, being obedient to the Spirit is how I was raised. I spoke with my grandma again and ended the call with "I am on my way over."

When I arrived, my mom was balled up on the bed, with a look of discomfort embedded all over her face. My sister had arrived also, only to diagnose the situation as her having trapped gas. "Girl, I don't think that much gas would cause this much pain. I'm taking her to the hospital." My sister shrugged and I heard my grandma quoting Scriptures for healing as we headed out the door. While driving, I asked my mom what she had eaten during the week. With a very weak voice she mumbled, "I have not eaten at all." I became a little worried. I was hoping maybe it was food poisoning; but, since she had not eaten, I wondered, "Now what's wrong?!" I quickly pulled up in front of the emergency room entrance to let her out first. We headed straight to check in, and after finding somewhere to sit, my mom and I started talking about the tons of people already there. We both said, "This is going to be a long night."

After completing the paperwork, I sent a few text messages to my fiancé, grandma, and sister letting each of them know we had arrived. Since my wedding was the next week, my mom and I talked about what color dress she could wear and what hairstyles to get. She's the mother of the bride, why wouldn't she need to look fierce?! A few minutes passed before we were called to the back. Coming from a family that NEVER went to the hospital, why would I expect the worst to happen? As the nurse escorted us to the room, she asked questions about the onset of the pain and if my mom ever had previous problems. Due to the pain my mom was in, I finished up the remaining paperwork that had been given to her. The first thing they had her do was urinate in a cup. The color of the urine was concerning, but my mom has always been a soda drinker with little to no water. I said to her, "This may be an issue with your kidneys, which can be cleared up in a few days." Since the urine was an unhealthy color, the physician on staff ordered a CT scan with contrast. Anyone that has never been to the hospital for near death situations would have no understanding of this terminology.

I asked the doctor why the CT scan with contrast was needed and how long it would take. He answered, "This will help me see a clearer picture of her abdomen and point out anything that is abnormal from the liquid that she drinks." The look on me and my mom's faces were, "If this will speed up the process, then let's get it done." After getting my mom prepped for the CT, I began making phone calls to my fiancé, sister, and grandma to keep them in the loop of what was happening. As I waited for my mom to return from the CT scan, I sat there praying that everything would be fine and we would soon be out of there. I said Isaiah 53:5 repeatedly, "But he was wounded for our transgressions, he was bruised for our iniquities: the chastisement of our peace was upon him; and with his stripes we are healed" (KJV). After

45 minutes, my mother returned and we waited an hour for the results. By that time, I was real antsy and still hoping for positive results. We had already been there for four hours.

The radiologist returned with the results of the CT scan. We were not expecting to hear the diagnosis we were about to receive. She said, "Well, Miss Harris. The CT scan doesn't look good, and from this we may have to perform emergency surgery. We will get a final decision when the physician returns." I instantly felt nauseous and the room began spinning. "Why would surgery be needed, what's wrong?!" I asked. The diagnoses that was given was gastrointestinal perforation, which is a ruptured bowel consisting of a hole in the abdominal wall. "She did have abdominal pain, but there are tons of non-severe situations that could cause abdominal pain," I thought to myself.

When the radiologist left the room, I started making calls. Since my grandma was older and it was late, I didn't want her to come. I told my sister, "When I receive more information and a definite answer, I will call you to come." My fiancé immediately jumped in the car and drove to the hospital. I tried to remain sane until we heard from the doctor, but with so much still left to do for my wedding, I immediately became overwhelmed. I asked my mom how she was feeling, and she was very surprised and confused as to what was taking place. My fiancé arrived at the same time the doctor was coming in. The doctor advised us that he would take a few minutes to review the results of the CT scan and give us the best options.

A few minutes later he said, "We will have to have the emergency surgery. I will place it on the chart, and get you prepped and fully admitted into a more comfortable room." I was barely running on fumes from lack of sleep, and this had literally become a nightmare. I told my mom the Lord would not put more on us than we can bare. I began encouraging her and trying to keep her positive. I was 100 percent sure this would be like a day surgery and she would be released within a few days. It was 4:30 a.m. and we were waiting for her to be transferred to one of the main rooms. I told her that I was going to the car to take a nap, and that Grandma would be arriving in the morning. My aunt that works at the hospital came to check on us from time to time, and she recommended the surgeon that would be performing the procedure. She informed the rest of the family about what had happened and to pray for healing and a quick recovery.

At 7:30 a.m. the next day, my grandma arrived. When I walked back into the hospital room, she was laying hands on my mother and speaking healing to her body. She is a true woman of God and a true believer in faith. The comfort and support from my fiancé was very much needed. It was finally time to transfer my mother to her own room where we all could be more comfortable.

Other family members came to visit. It took a lot to make me leave because I did not want to miss anything that was said or done. I sat at the house and continued to pray for healing and for a quick turnaround in her recovery. While looking at the ceiling I said, "Lord, I need you now more than I have ever needed you before. My wedding is next week, and my mom has to be there!" It was a little after 12 p.m. when I received a call from my grandma that they would soon be prepping my mother for surgery at no later than 2 p.m. Thankfully it was during the summer, so I didn't have to worry about my children getting to and from school.

We arrived back at the hospital just a little before the nurses were bringing my mother down for the surgery. The look on my mom's face was heartbreaking; she looked so nervous. We gathered all the family members that were present and said a powerful prayer to ease her mind. After they took her to the back, we all gathered in the waiting room to begin counting down the time for the procedure. It was so stressful just to think about the risk of possible side effects, such as: slipping into a comma or even death. The only thing that was going through my mind was, "What if I lose my mother during a time that should be filled with happiness instead of the pain right now?" As much as I trust in God, I needed a 911 in this situation. It was June 11, 2015, and my wedding was set for June 20. I had so much going on in my head between last-minute wedding jitters and the outcome of my mom's surgery. I just couldn't understand why this was happening now. My aunt who works at the hospital checked in from time to time to provide us with updates.

A fast recovery is exactly what I had been praying for. "Now we just need to get past the rehab," I thought to myself. As soon as the surgery was completed, my mom would be transferred to the recovery room where she would need to be for at least an hour. However, we did get to see her during the transfer. She was still heavily sedated and wasn't aware of what was going on and who was there. I looked at the clock and it was 6 p.m. The staff had just gotten her to the room, she was barely moving due to the pain, and the medication was wearing off. My sister brought my kids to see her and it was too much for her to handle because she immediately became nauseous and vomited. There were so many tubes going into her and a lot of machines making beeping noises.

After being in the hospital for four days, her recovery wasn't coming along well. She was not able to eat solid foods at all and she could only drink the liquids that were given to her through a tube. They kept one down her throat to suction out the infection and fluids. I prayed, "But He was wounded for our transgressions, He was bruised for our iniquities; the chastisement of our peace was upon Him; and with His stripes she is healed." It was five days until my wedding and I was a wreck. I was learning that something like this could happen to anyone. Only God could pull her through and we had to trust Him. Keeping faith and having support was going to help the outcome of the situation. Each day seemed to get harder and harder. We were hearing from the doctors that she would not make it to my wedding because the drainage was not letting up, she had a fever, and her sugar was low. One of the nicest nurses said a prayer for my mom and told her that if she hadn't come to the hospital within two days of her arrival, she would have died at home.

If I hadn't been obedient to the Spirit when I was led to bring her to the hospital, I would have not only been having my wedding but a funeral as well. As my mom continued to get visitors, I had some time to step away and clear my head by doing last minute wedding shopping. Anyone that has ever been married or is getting married knows there is a lot of chaos and stress. I was at Ross looking for shoes for my daughter when my sister called to give me some unwanted news. "They said Momma is not going to be out in time for your wedding, she's not recovering fast enough." I couldn't do anything but cry, I didn't know who to blame; it just wasn't fair! We had been informed that a second surgery would take place. As difficult and painful as it was for my mom, we were not agreeing to a second surgery. We needed to hear from God.

After attending the wedding rehearsal, it became real that my mom wouldn't be there. The day of the wedding was such a rush, no one seemed to be concerned that she wasn't present. Even though I felt pain on the inside, I kept a huge smile on the outside. The photographer managed to catch photos of me on FaceTime with my mom as I was getting ready. After the reception, we all headed to the hospital to see my mom. We received a lot of attention because we were still dressed in our wedding attire. I did not want to miss getting a picture with her on that day. The joy in her eyes was indescribable, but I could also see the hurt and disappointment she felt from not being at the wedding.

I could hear her faintly say, "I'm sorry I couldn't make it to the wedding." By this time, I fully gave it to God. I knew it was part of His plan and this was all happening for a reason. Two months later—after three surgeries, the removal of her gallbladder, and physical rehab—the doctors finally fixed the torn bowl and she was released. My advice to anyone that has gone through or is going through a similar situation is to trust God! He is a way maker, He is a doctor in the sickroom, and He is worthy of all the glory. God does not make mistakes, He is all knowing and all powerful!

SOUL REFLECTION:
Have you identified your core values and written a personal mission to achieve your desired goals? What are the essential elements in your life that allow for an ongoing relationship with God and spiritual strength?

Self-Love: Loving Yourself Is Seeing Yourself the Way God Sees You!

SONYA SCOTT

"How can you believe, when you receive glory from one another and you do not seek the glory that is from the one and only God?"

—John 5:44 (NASB)

It's so easy for us in our human nature to let others or society tell us who we are, who we should be, and who we should aspire to become. We try to fit into a puzzle of perfection that is next to impossible. Because of this mindset, we are overlooking the person God called and created us to be. To our own detriment, whether we know it or not, we're taking the true essence of who God created and locking him or her in a closet. God's creation is banging on the door and screaming that we let him or her out, but we dismiss who we are every time we try to pursue endeavors that are not true to our calling, act outside of our character, or put on a façade that we're something or someone that we're not. By constantly trying to transform into someone or something God did not create us to be, we are subconsciously dismissing Him by telling ourselves that He (a God who does not make mistakes) made a mistake when He created us. Instead of going to Him and asking Him to reveal to us how He sees us and perfecting ourselves in Him, we seek to be a reflection of "worldly" approval. I know this because I used to live this way not really knowing that I was. I thought that I had everything under control until everything started to spiral out of control! I got to a point where I didn't really know who I was because I spent so much time trying to be who everyone else wanted and needed me to be. It was like I woke up one day and had no direction and no true identity.

My journey to seeing myself the way that God sees me and seeing myself as the woman He created me to be started with a dream that I had about four years ago. The dream changed my relationship with God and started me on the path of self-discovery. I gained a newfound confidence and an appreciation for the woman He created me to be.

In my dream, I was standing in a long line of people in a dimly lit room. I didn't know why we were standing in this line and I didn't know any of the people that I was standing in line with. I couldn't see that far ahead of me, and for some reason I never looked back to see how many people were behind me. There was no sense of time, so I didn't have that impatient feeling like I had to hurry up to get to the front of the line quickly. I was more curious about why I was in this line and what would be waiting for me when I got to the front of it. As I got closer to the front of the line, I noticed that everyone standing in the line was being presented with the most beautifully lit spheres. The closer I got, the spheres looked more like glowing orbs and each orb was a different color. There were red, green, yellow, orange, violet, and pink orbs, all of which were more vibrantly colored than I had ever seen. They were absolutely beautiful! I started to become more excited the closer I got to the front of the line. Although I still wasn't sure what these orbs were or why they were being given, they were so beautiful that I didn't really care at that point, I just wanted one.

When I arrived at the front of the line, there was a table with various colored orbs on the right and left side of it. However, there was one brilliantly orange colored orb at the center of the table that seemed to have a glow to it. Something inside of me told me that the orb had been placed at the center of the table specifically for me. As I reached to pick it up, I heard a voice. The voice was very calming and comforting and I instantly knew that the voice was God's. What He said to me in that moment changed my mindset and the way that I felt about Him and myself.

God told me that all of the orbs on the table represented all of the blessings He has been waiting to give to me. He told me that He has been with me all along, waiting and holding them for me. He kept asking me why I had not come to Him to receive them yet. In my heart, I knew that He was asking me this question to make me think about it and be honest with Him, but I couldn't answer. I was trying to speak, but no words would come out of my mouth. God showed me all of the people who were in line with me happily receiving their blessings in the form of these orbs. They were leaving the table with more blessings, in a multitude of colors, than they could possibly carry. God then guided me to pick up the orange orb, the blessing that He had for me at the center of the table, and told me to keep it and cherish it. He told me that when I was ready, the rest of my blessings would still be there waiting for me and He would be there waiting to give them to me.

This dream was so vivid that when I woke up, I had tears in my eyes and almost didn't know where I was. In the days following, as I reflected on my dream, the question that God asked me kept playing in my head. Why had I not come to Him to receive my blessings? It became clear to me that I had been looking for what God already had for me, all I needed to do was develop a deeper relationship with Him. I realized that my true identity would only be found in God.

> "And the one on whom seed was sown on the good soil, this is the man who hears the word and understands it; who indeed bears fruit and brings forth, some a hundredfold, some sixty, and some thirty."
>
> —Matthew 13:23 (NASB)

Days went by, and I could not get the dream that I had out of my head. I kept seeing the brightly colored orange orb in my mind and started searching to find out the biblical meaning of the color orange. I found that there are several meanings for the color orange, but the one that really stuck with me and touched my heart is that the color orange often symbolizes harvest. After reading Matthew 13:18-23, I realized that I was not sowing God's Word in my life properly and therefore what God had sown in my heart when He created me was not being watered and nurtured. I had failed to harvest His Word, so much so that I lost sight of how much God really loved me. By doing that, I unknowingly let the enemy snatch my God-given identity.

When I had this dream, I was at a point in my life where I had been through so much disappointment and hurt that whenever anything good happened to me, I expected something bad to happen. I was tired of trying to control everything and everyone around me. I did not know it then, but I now realize that I would try to please everyone in order to control their opinion of me. I didn't want anyone to see that I was broken, so I put on a mask like everything was okay. I was afraid of making mistakes, so instead of stepping out on faith and pursuing what God was leading me to pursue, I did what everyone else thought I should do so that if something went wrong I wouldn't look like a complete failure and I would have others to blame. I was miserable and trying to live a life that was not my own, not only in my personal life but in my career as well. Instead of trusting God and planting seeds of faith by walking boldly as a victor in His calling, I was victimizing myself by trying to live up to worldly standards.

I started praying with more purpose and being more transparent with God. My prayers became more of a counseling session with Him and I started trusting Him more each time that I prayed. I used to think that some of the things I went through that were hurtful and disappointing was God punishing me for something that I had done wrong. But the more I opened up to God, He revealed to me that I was going through these things so that I would seek Him for guidance in order to establish a deeper relationship with Him. Through talking to God, I learned that I needed to see Him for the true essence of who He is so that I could visualize and become the true essence of who He created me to be.

As my relationship with God deepened, He started to show me who I really was and the things that I was doing at that stage in my life that were causing barriers in our relationship. It wasn't that I didn't believe in God, or that I didn't pray daily, or even that I didn't have faith because I did. What God revealed to me was that I was holding everything inside and that I was trying to look perfect in His eyes in the same way that I was trying to look perfect in man's eyes. I was doing this in vain because God sees all things and knows me better than I know myself.

He guided me to Scriptures that spoke about the dangers of hiding who I was from Him and how doing this changed my relationship with Him.

> "Then the eyes of both of them were opened, and they knew that they were naked; and they sewed fig leaves together and made themselves loin coverings. They heard the sound of the LORD God walking in the garden in the cool of the day, and the man and his wife hid themselves from the presence of the LORD God among the trees of the garden. Then the LORD God called to the man, and said to him, 'Where are you?' He said, 'I heard the sound of You in the garden, and I was afraid because I was naked; so I hid myself.'"
>
> —Genesis 3:7-10 (NASB)

These Scriptures in Genesis give the same message that Jesus gave in His parable about the sower of seeds. If we don't understand God's Word and have unwavering faith in Him, we won't have a healthy relationship with Him. Then, the enemy can trick us and steal the identity God gave us. As a result, our wavering faith in God changes how we view our relationship with Him; but, He doesn't change. He still sees us as who He created us to be. After reading those Scriptures, I got my first glimpse of seeing myself as God created me. I was uncovered with no secrets or masks and standing strong in my faith in Him.

Today, I have more confidence, I'm happier than I have been in a long time, I have peace, and I have a clear vision of God's purpose and calling on my life. I no longer seek approval from other people. Instead, I seek God's approval and move forward boldly in what He calls me to do. I have learned that when I used to hide myself and try to be who everyone else wanted me to be, not only was I hindering my own blessings, but I was also hindering the blessings of those who God had called me to be a blessing to. I have been so blessed over these past four years that I am overwhelmed with joy and humbled to know that God loves me so much that He trusts me to serve His people. I have seen God work in ways that I have not experienced before, not only for myself but also in the lives of others. I have truly been touched and inspired. Things that I would have overlooked before, I see clearly now, and I know that it's only because of my renewed relationship with God.

We live in a world where a lot is expected of us. We're expected to be everything to everyone, hold down a lucrative career, have all the answers, be the best spouse in the world, be the best parent in the world, and maintain an image of perfection while doing all of these things. We don't owe the world anything, but we owe God everything. However, God only expects that we love, seek, trust, receive Him, and love each other. God will show us exactly who He created us to be and how we are to live out the calling He has placed on our lives. He is the only one who can love us through all of our mistakes and failures and see the beauty in all of our scars and imperfections. I am encouraging you to seek Him first and find love for yourself through the love He has for you.

SOUL REFLECTION:
As my relationship with God grows, I am loving and seeing myself the way God loves and sees me. I no longer seek "worldly" approval as to whether or not I'm good enough, strong enough, smart enough, or worthy enough. I know that I am because God is telling me so!

His Sins, My Journey

WINDI FLOYD REYNOLDS

But they that wait upon the LORD shall renew their strength; they shall mount up with wings as eagles; they shall run, and not be weary; and they shall walk, and not faint."

—Isaiah 40:31 (KJV)

Have you ever wondered why bad things always seem to happen to you? Or perhaps why all the goodness that is life just doesn't seem to happen as it should for you? My dad once told me that bad things would happen to me for all the wrong that he had done in his life. The concept never left me, and in my youth, I waited on the worst to happen. I walked through my youthful days expecting the deficiencies, waiting for the unwanted circumstances and neglect to occur. I accepted and believed in a mediocre standard of myself. I clung to what appeared like love at the time but was just men who wanted nothing more than sex. I moved through life merely just existing. It's weird because when I think back, I would say during my youth I didn't have the drive to do more than just exist. I mean, what else was there for me to do outside of just existing when I didn't have anything to look forward to other than the looming delinquent debt I owed to karma thanks to my dad?

Most of us as children envision what our lives will become. You know, the feeling you have as a kid thinking of what you want to be when you grow up. For me, I never really thought too hard about what was to come. As a teenager, I mostly just went with the flow from day to day. Again, just existing and waiting for the expected doom to occur that had been predestined over my life as my dad had warned me. As I aged into my twenties, life started to slow a bit and I began to put more thought into my actions. I started to lean on and look to God for answers that I couldn't find within myself. Actually, I started to put extreme thought into everything I did. I would overthink and overanalyze my every action and I would pray about it.

During this period of my life, I began to pray more than ever. I think back on all the times I reached out to God with a call for help, a call to turn my current situation around: "Lord, if you get me out of this situation, I promise..." "God, please help me land this job." "Lord, don't let this happen to me." "God, please show me that this man is the one for me." Then, I would wait for God to answer my call. My thought process was if I prayed hard enough, it would happen. So, you can imagine that since this was my logic, my prayers were often. I had it all figured out.

When I was good (meaning: when I was a good person and acted in accordance with what most Christians would consider to be right), good would in turn come my way. Also, in the reverse, when bad things happened in my life, they happened because it was God's way of punishing me for doing something wrong. When I reflect on my life during that period of my journey, the process of praying and waiting on God to answer my prayers was a common theme. Although I consistently prayed for favor, nothing seemed to quite go my way. I often wondered about God and His ability to shape my life. I wondered if others were asking for the same things as me because, for the most part, we all want similar things out of life: happiness, success, and so forth. I questioned what makes the trajectory of each person's life so different despite constant calls to God to change our circumstances.

Throughout my twenties, I experienced broken hearts, failed relationships, financial difficulty, and years of bouncing from college to college—unfocused and unable to graduate, which in turn garnered me a career that was going absolutely nowhere. However, I continued to reach out to God in hopes that He would bring something new, a burst of life where for years there had not been one. I prayed and waited. Finally, in 2006, it was only God Himself that got me to return to my hometown and I started on a path of excellence while attending Savannah State University. Finally, in May of 2009 (ten long years after graduating from high school), I graduated from college. I was the first in my immediate family to graduate from college. I graduated summa cum laude in the top seven of my graduating class at Savannah State University. I was above the moon about the achievement. I was banking on the fact that since I had completed an internship with the Savannah Music Festival, working with their public relations manager, it would help me in my job search. The days, weeks, and months after graduation, I continuously prayed to God to send a job my way. I prayed for direction because the days of me believing that I was destined for a horrid life were behind me. Forget about what my dad had instilled in me, I had my God, and my heavenly Father had the answer to my prayers. So, I prayed and I applied. I prayed and applied. Ultimately, although I fervently prayed and held a college degree, not one employer called with an offer of employment.

During the course of the year following graduation, I was continuously rejected by every job I applied for. I didn't understand what was going on and why I wasn't getting called back. Instead of calls, I received a continuous stream of "Thank you for applying. Better luck next time" emails. So, I decided to return to school for a master's degree. With my master's degree I was almost guaranteed to land a job. Right? In 2010, I reenrolled in school and started the journey to receive my graduate degree. The process of graduate school was painstaking because I was unfulfilled with my current circumstances all while trying to refocus my mind on being a student again. Nevertheless, by 2012, I received my master's degree and again I was beyond proud of myself. I was excited yet again about the endless opportunities I had in front of me. I felt that things were on their way to being different!

After graduation, I continued to call upon God. Once again, I applied, prayed, and waited. I applied, prayed, and waited. Still, rejection was around every corner. The waiting continued for years. The wait consisted of me applying and waiting for God to send the perfect job my way. It seemed so easy for some. Why was it so difficult for me? In my stillness, I began to reflect deeply and wonder about what my dad had told me long ago. Maybe this was karma's way of catching up with me and causing me to pay for all the wrongs he had done in his life. This had to be true because was I not worthy of a chance? Although I had put in the time, effort, and prayers, things in my life were still not shifting in the way I needed them to. I began to wonder if God was even listening to me. Inwardly, this was a disappointing time in my life but outwardly I kept up a good appearance of being okay with my bleak circumstances.

    A lot of time passed, but one day after taking in some much-needed advice and growing tired of wallowing in self-pity, a light went off and I had an epiphany of sorts. Maybe I was going about this thing called life all wrong. Over the years, I had simplified life to right and wrong. You do good and good happens in return. You do bad and bad happens. I applied that concept to every aspect of my life, including my job search, because I truly thought that you should have no problems finding work and being successful when you have a degree and you pray about it! Oh, my. I had managed to turn God into a simple creator versus all the complexity that is Him. I realized it was not about me sitting and waiting on God, it was about me relying on Him to guide me as I worked through each challenge life threw my way. It wasn't about the wait, it was about the work. I wasn't supposed to wait on God to make things happen. God expected me to be a willing participant in the process.

To Wait vs. To Require

To wait is to stay where one is until a particular time or until something else happens.

Translation to God: I have received my degrees and now I am praying to You and waiting on You to send the perfect job my way.

To require is to instruct or expect someone to do something.

Translation to Self: Don't wait on Him. Require much of self.

I think we all wait on God to send us so much—a job, a man, or better life circumstances. But, what are we requiring from ourselves to get us the very things we desire, want, and need out of life? As the challenges come our way, what are we requiring from ourselves to take us where we need to be? Are we using God as a crutch or as a guide? Personally, while I was in college all those years, I completed the hours needed to get my degrees, but I still hadn't completed the personal work and hours needed to prepare myself for what was needed after I received them. I had not had the serious conversation with myself to ask, "Where are you going and what are the steps needed to get there?" I did not follow through with a plan.

You see, I thought God was supposed to direct me and answer all the burning questions I had inside. I thought God was supposed to show me a sign. All those years I had prayed for direction and answers from God, and He was directing and answering me all along. He was directing me toward all the answers that were within me. From birth, God had already equipped me with the tools of self-sufficiency. I had made the transition from believing what my dad had told me all those years ago and being held down for his wrongs to relying on God. However, my reliance on God was my fallback as to why things weren't going my way. So, even as a young adult (just as in my youth), I was walking through life merely existing and without a purpose.

SOUL REFLECTION:
I had faith in God, but no faith in myself. I was praying to God, but not requiring enough of myself. I was walking through life expecting a result from God when life does not work that way. God does not work that way. God didn't owe me an answer. I owed Him. So, I altered my way of thinking and instead of always asking God for something, I started to continuously thank Him for my blessings. I thanked Him for taking me through the trials and tribulations. I thanked Him for helping me through the rough and tough times, because in those times was when I became the most enlightened. I realized it wasn't God or another person's fault that I was in the situation I was in. I had to grab ahold of my life and stop making excuses for all the things going on that I didn't want. I had to realize it wasn't God that would change this for me. God put the power and strength inside of me from creation to be able to tackle the challenges that would come my way. And even in those times when I was not equipped to face certain challenges, God had already instilled in me the know-how to start from nothing and create something

amazing. It wasn't God's duty to place anything in my lap, it was my duty to put in the work and require myself to use the tools God so graciously equipped me with from the start.

Looking back on my earliest memories, God has had my back since the beginning of my story. To know me from the start is to understand my present and to see into my future. If I start from the beginning, that's where the soul of my story begins, somewhere between light and darkness.

Training Day

DENESHA MANNING

"But God is doing what is best for us, training us to live God's holy best. At the time, discipline isn't much fun. It always feels like it's going against the grain. Later, of course, it pays off handsomely, for it's the well-trained who find themselves mature in their relationship with God."

—Hebrews 12:10-11 (MSG)

Bupropion XL tablets used to treat depression. Lexapro used to treat depression and anxiety. Restoril (Temazepam) used to treat insomnia. Klonopin (Clonazepam) is a sedative used to treat panic disorder and anxiety. All of these medications were prescribed to me in one visit after speaking with a psychiatrist in May 2017. Within only a few minutes of me sharing my occupational story, she was engulfed in the warfare surrounding me. She leaned back, then pressed forward, removing her glasses, then readjusting them to her face. Her clinical mind took a backseat to the shear amazement of the words spoken out of the mouth of a young, unmarried woman who endured seven years of constant turmoil. How could this soft, youthful-faced young lady with a southern accent be in her right mind? The thought that I had to wrestle with life on my own was beyond her belief, so much so, that she even referred me to a psychologist because in her opinion, additional ongoing guidance *should be* needed.

The psychiatrist asked me over and over, "Have you ever had suicidal thoughts?" The question rattled me. Before I could answer her, she took her pen and feverishly began scribbling on her prescription pad. Her clinical brain flipped a switch. She instructed me to take this pill for immediate relief, this pill for extended relief, this pill for quick onset, this pill for sleep, this pill for rising, and the list goes on and on. I didn't set the appointment for medicine, I just needed to spill my guts to someone who I could confide in. What was my response to her question? I asked her, "Have you ever had suicidal thoughts?"

All of us who believe in Jesus Christ as our Lord and Savior have at least one spiritual gift. Some have more than one. Let us not be jealous or envious of those who may have been imparted additional gifts by the Holy Spirit because to whom much is given, much is required. I never imagined that the training ground God would place me in to illuminate my gifts, stir them up, and ultimately manifest them would be a corporate environment. When my prayers were broken down to moans and groans or one-letter words like, "When?" "How long?" "Why?" or "I need you," I knew God was breaking me down to total dependency on Him. But, I had to be developed.

As a Veteran who endured Basic Training, the Army didn't just give me an M-16 rifle and say, "Here, now use it." No, I had to be trained and tested. And after multiple evaluations, I was trusted to effectively utilize the weapon that was gifted to me. I reached out to people, they pushed back. I thought to myself, "David had Jonathan. Ruth had Naomi. Joshua had Caleb. Moses had Aaron. Can a Sista get some help?" I'm not talking about a seasonal friend, battle buddy, or temporary mentor. I wanted a lifelong assignment. And while I was asking Jesus, "Can I have a husband?" my father who was a man of faith and leadership passed away. My great-grandmother, the spiritual reference of my life passed away. My dog died, friends stripped and pruned away. Stress was wreaking havoc on my body and I began to have issues with my health. Thankfully, I had my mom and a few supporters who prayed for me, but God said, "That's it." What I was asking for during what seemed like hell and perpetual loss is what He used to guide me into a relationship with Him. Seeking Him through the pain, shame, hurt, isolation, persecution, rejection, lying, and backstabbing was His curriculum for training. As He got me to Himself, He was delighted. I must admit, at the time, it didn't feel good at all to me! However, the blessing was that for the first time, He could ask me, "Can you hear me now?" and I could respond with a resounding, "Yes!"

    Now, hearing from God is great, but why is it useful? Manipulators come in all shapes, forms, and sizes. Some are not as easily discerned as others. Where there are spirits of Jezebel and Ahab, your eyes and ears need fine-tuning. Jealousy and envy can creep up on us in the form of friends. Leaders can seem well intentioned while attempting to play with our livelihood as if it is a simple game of chess. For those of us who want to give people the benefit of the doubt, this can be disheartening. I trusted the wrong people. My integrity was challenged by those who shared my race. I was ostracized because I wouldn't go along with the crowd while being forced to choose between right and wrong. Sitting alone for years with no one to confide in, yet, still faithfully serving and worshipping God in the midst of trouble became my norm. I had ample opportunities to give up. I couldn't. There was this undeniable Force that kept whispering in my ear. His voice kept reminding me that He was my protector. How could I know that unless I was in trouble? And boy, was I in trouble! He made everybody hate me! I couldn't phone a friend at work even if I had to. Heaven was rejoicing; but, I was holding on to God's hand so tightly that if He could bruise, I'm sure I left an imprint! Every meeting was an opportunity for the Holy Spirit to comfort me in my isolation and rejection. In the midst of it all, I noticed something. My spiritual eyes and ears were operating at a heightened sense of awareness. I had visions and dreams—I saw what was driving those around me. I learned how to pray. I mean really pray. I went deeper in God.

On the side of the highway, leaving a meeting in Austin, Texas, I was baptized in the Holy Spirit. While listening to a message from a well-known pastor, I sat in my car having a moment with the Holy Spirit that I can never fully explain. My mouth started speaking in a foreign tongue, and I felt a wind lifting me higher. After I gathered myself, I realized that this experience came after multiple attempts to undermine my performance, discriminatory practices that could potentially limit my growth, and several failed attempts to break my spirit through malicious actions and slanderous words. And as a reward for my faithfulness, in spite of the distractions, I continued to exceed expectations. God kept reminding me that everything in our lives is seasonal. The enemies that I saw before, I would not see them again. I held on to this particular word, praying for a speedy deliverance. But to my surprise, victory led to the next challenge. God is our protector, the battle is not ours; however, we must stand and diligently seek Him in order to experience His victory. I came to the realization that people were not fighting me. The enemy was fighting what God was doing in me. Praying in the Spirit was God's plan. Circumstances drove me deeper and deeper into His bosom. The training continued, and the plot thickened. "What's next, Father?" I asked. He responded, "Forgiveness." I responded, "Lord, I have to forgive?" His answer was, "Yes."

"I know I've been changed" (in my singing voice) was my next test. I was still single and in my mess. I was thankful for all of those who were holding up their rod while I was fighting on the battlefield of faith, but the truth of the matter is that we feel very alone during these perpetual seasons of testing. I even got to the point where I would, and still do at times, sleep in my prayer closet. I withstood it all—from the attempts to destroy my reputation, demoting me, and pressuring me to give up and quit. Things got really heated when human resources knew me by name, and I was called in. I thought, "God, you want me to forgive after all of this?" I have faith, vision, a prophetic tongue, a discerning spirit, wisdom, and understanding like a seasoned sage, isn't that enough? I've been leading as a subordinate, shouldn't I receive a gold star for that? I haven't denied my Jesus and I made it clear that I am Your servant to everyone around me." "Deliver me from this mess" was my prayer. I tore the church up worshipping Him. I loved on people that despitefully used me. I changed, Lord, I changed. But forgiveness was the key.

No matter what, I had to forgive. God wanted me to not look at those that challenged my faith as enemies, but to view them as friends. Yes, they were all simply my friends. You see, the battle is not about us. God was demonstrating His ability to use this limited vessel for His glory. How can we be powerful, anointed leaders without forgiveness? Moses couldn't see the Promised Land with resentment and anger, so neither could I. God gave me a strategy! I sat in my car next to evil month after month. I knew the devil hated praise and worship music, so I blasted my gospel music during every field ride. I made sure to give God the glory every step of the way. I took things a step further and began praying for those who hurt me. I knew God transformed me at this point. As maturity set in, my spiritual eyes began to see what was hidden behind their evil. Some had difficult pasts from different forms of abuse, others had hidden sins that were buried for years, and I even saw childhood abandonment driving these "friends" to pursue evil instead of good. The Bible says that in all thy getting get understanding. The understanding was the anesthesia that I needed to take the sting out of my situation.

I heard the saying, "Hurt people, hurt people." It's true. In the midst of it all, I witnessed angels. I'm not lying. God spoke through so many people during my journey. The time had come where I knew I was being prepared to cut the umbilical cord of my past and move forward to entrepreneurship. My heart opened up to the possibilities of taking everything I learned in corporate America and transforming myself into the owner I was created to be. After a total of 11 years, I finally aligned myself with God's will. I heard Pastor Bill Winston say, "When you ask the Holy Spirit the right question, He'll always respond."

In July 2017, I prayed. I said, "Father, my assignment at this company is over. I've fought the good fight of faith, forgiven my enemies, declared your name in darkness, and I'm ready to come out." I knew God was calling me to entrepreneurship. During all of the turmoil, believe it or not, I had notebooks full of research and plans for businesses. There were years of material gathered, but I never moved forward because I had not broken the yoke off my life. I continued asking God to bring me out with great substance like the children of Israel. In three months, God answered my prayers! He is my provider. The training continued.

God answered my prayers in the form of a layoff! Yes, a layoff! From the moment I prayed in July 2017 to October 2017, I worked extensively on my business, Fashioned4Dominion, LLC. I contacted my trademark attorney, had photo shoots, and created strategies based on my years of research. I launched my website in October 2017, and later that month, I unexpectedly received a layoff notice. I shouted with a voice of triumph! It was one of those moments where I knew I was really operating in God's plan. Everything, and I do mean everything, lined up for me. My Father ensured that I would be well taken care of during my transition. My debts were paid. I would continue having benefits and pay through the year 2018 and I had access to other financial sources as well. I've been soaring ever since! I prayed and asked God for spiritual covering and mentors. I wanted people in my life who had been tried and tested. People who loved Jesus and would have my best interest at the forefront of their minds. God sent Russ and Cheryl Polote-Williamson. As a result of God's faithfulness, I've become an actress in a stage play. Fashioned4Dominion, LLC is flourishing and I'm gaining exposure via modeling and speaking. God bestowed me with excellent friends who pray for me and cheer me on in my pursuit of living a life with purpose and joy. My body is stronger and healing from the scars of stress. I realized that all of the prophets and those called to do great things had to endure years of what seemed like a wilderness in order to walk into their Promised Land. I made many mistakes along the way, but the seven-year transformation into who I am today is nothing short of a miracle.

My suggestion to anyone who God is going to use in a profound way is to understand that He's training you. It's not about the people around you. It's not even about the mistakes that you've made. It's about Him developing you from the inside out in an effort to have an intimate relationship with you. One thing I know for sure is that when I do things God's way, He always blesses me exceedingly, abundantly, above all that I may ask or think! I trust Him. I'm looking forward to having a beautiful family to continue my legacy of faith. Stay tuned!

So, to answer the initial question, "Was I suicidal?" the answer is a resounding, "No!" I was tired and maybe even depressed, but not suicidal. When I left the psychiatrist's office that day in May 2017, I was speechless. I slowly walked into my home. I stood still for a moment in my kitchen. All of a sudden, I started running through my living room praising God! I realized what the psychiatrist couldn't figure out was how I had not considered taking my life after all that I had been through. But she didn't know my secret... the power of God can override any storm. The Holy Spirit is my friend and companion. My angels are my warriors. Most of all, Jesus is my Savior. Armed with the spiritual armor that I need, pills were never necessary nor were they ever taken. I filled the prescriptions as evidence to share that no weapon formed against me will ever prosper. Now, I can say with confidence that I can do all things through Christ which strengthens me.

SOUL REFLECTION:
There's not a person in this world that can hinder our ascension. "For promotion cometh neither from the east, nor from the west, nor from the south. But God is the judge: he putteth down one, and setteth up another."—Psalm 75:6-7 (KJV). We often give people or even the enemy too much credit when God is using them as tools to sharpen, mold, and design us into the people He created us to be. It is our perception that determines whether we are victors or victims. What we gain along the journey of faith is far more potent and beneficial than a title or a bump in our income. It is the intimacy with the Almighty God that calls us into kingdom living and thinking. As spectators watch our faith in motion, they are inclined to ask about the Jesus we serve. It is not our sob story that makes people whisper at us in

the dark and ask, "What must I do to be saved?" Nor is it miracles. If miracles were all that it took for people to want to come to Christ, then the children of Israel would've been completely sold out! But when we witness faith in motion, our lives are forever changed. It's never about us. It is about God loving us through His forms of training to bring us to a place of intimacy, unshakeable faith, and love.

If You FIGHT, the Devil Can't Win
WINIFRED "TEDDI" JONES

"For the Lord your God is he that goeth with you, to fight for you against your enemies, to save you."

—Deuteronomy 20:4 (KJV)

It seems as though I lived a life that if I whispered a prayer God would answer me within minutes. I would pray for or about everything that was going on with me and immediately know my next move, until that dreadful day that my faith in Him was tested and became almost nonexistent for a while. After years of declaring, "My God is my everything!" my faith was shaken, broken, and lost amongst pieces of scattered pain.

On February 25, 2010, I made a conscious decision to petition my Father in Heaven for guidance concerning my purpose and the kind of woman He wanted me to be. You see, I was at an impasse. Divorced after being married for many years to an abusive man, raising two teens on my own, working crazy hours as a nurse at the county jail while trying to be that devout Christian attending church and participating in praise dance combined with other ministry outings had me in a perplexed mode. I pretended to be happy every day. I pretended that the exit from a loveless marriage didn't hurt and that being alone was a wonderful way to live my life. So, on that day, I started what I thought would be the easiest journey to my destination.

I decided it was time to fast and pray. Lying in my bed with my Bible, journal, and favorite pen, I was ready to receive a word from God. While praying and dozing off after doing 16 hours of work the night before, I heard a knock at my door. Not sure if it was the door or something going on outside, I ignored it. It came again, only this time it was louder. In my head I was thinking, "No one knows I am home, I am not opening it." The third time it was so loud that I jumped out of bed with a force that resembled the effects of a hard shove. I glanced at the clock that showed 12:05 in the afternoon, as I turned to look down the hall. That is when I saw three masked figures breaking the door off the hinges, entering my home with force, and heading straight toward me. I froze in fear as I was still trying to shake off the sleep. In disbelief, I was pushed hard against the wall by a male with a bandana that covered his face from his chin up to his eyes. He immediately put a .357 magnum between my eyes and asked if anyone was in the house with me. I told him no and he hit me in the mouth with the gun. He asked another question that I could barely hear. He wanted to know where my money was. I told him I had none. The next part I don't remember at all; but, from the crime scene photographs, I was beaten and dragged to my room. I woke up in between my bed and armoire and immediately got into a squatting position. The masked gunman started yelling at me to lay on my stomach, but I was too scared to move. He turned away very agitated, but kept the gun pointed at me as he shouted orders to the others on what to take.

When I thought I had a chance, I grabbed my cell phone from under the pillow, dialed 911, and threw my phone under the bed. With thoughts on how to escape running through my head, I could vaguely hear a voice in the distance saying, "This is 911. State your emergency." I realized that it was coming from my phone. Afraid that the intruders would hear the operator, I began to make noises. This angered the gunman who walked back in the room and pushed me down. He told me several times, "Don't make me hurt you, Ma'am." He started to walk away as the sound of the 911 operator seemed to amplify by 10! He turned, looked down, and saw the phone at the foot of the bed. I did not realize that I had thrown it that far, but I immediately predicted what happened next. He picked up the phone, saw that 911 had been called, and turned toward me while shouting at the others that the police were on their way. Then, he stepped outside the room and pointed the gun directly at me and released four shots back to back without hesitation. I dived for the door as one bullet entered my thigh. I slammed the door and three more bullets came through it. One hit the armoire, the others hit the floor and the wall. As I stood there shaking, I had no idea I had been hit until moments later when I could feel the blood running down my leg.

The police arrived after what seemed to have been an eternity, but I was told it was only 12 minutes from the time I called. They walked in with guns drawn, shouting at me to get on the floor. I told them I was the owner and that I lived there. By that time, I was feeling weak, cold, and tired. The paramedics grabbed me as I started to fall and lowered me to the floor. They immediately became fully aware that I had been shot in my left thigh. While they were working on me, I lost consciousness. What followed is blank until I woke up in the ER. I was treated, kept for a few hours and released, only to return a few days later with a serious infection from the gunshot wound.

I was thankful to be alive, but I wanted answers from God as to why He allowed this to happen to me. But, He gave me no answer! I asked again and again... no answer! I became increasingly angry and almost belligerent with God, but still... no answer.

I started my road to physical recovery, which was not easy since I was on crutches and not able to work, drive, or attend church. Praise dancing has always been my release to connect with God. It had gotten me through other tough situations, but it was totally impossible at this time. I was mentally and spiritually headed for destruction!

I was lost! The intruders had taken everything including my will to live. One of the worst side effects of a trauma like mine is reliving it daily, trying to figure out what you did to deserve it or how the outcome could be different. I could no longer enter a hospital without the smell of blood making me gag. I couldn't even do what I had done for years, which was nursing; it was a wrap. I tried to get help, but many doors were shut in my face. I was treated like the enemy instead of the victim. My talks with God became angry rants of rage. I wanted the physical and mental pain to go away. I wanted to die! All I could see was that the devil was winning, and

God was watching it happen. I stopped praying, reading my Bible, and believing. Suicide seemed to be the best option.

One day during one of my many pity parties, a deep sadness set in and I felt the weight of a big boulder sitting on my chest. I became very tired and sleepy. I sat quietly in my small room and I heard a voice say, "FIGHT! You are a fighter, so fight. I have chosen you for this journey, you must fight!" I started to cry. I screamed out as loud as I could, "I have no need to fight! You left me. You allowed them to hurt me!" With tears streaming down my face so heavily that my clothes became soaked, I had no strength to fight. I was filled with so much animosity and bitterness, it seemed that no one, I mean NO ONE, would or could help me. My children, church, and friends tried, and I went to counselors, but nothing changed.

Nine months had passed and I had lost everything that the intruders left. I was homeless, jobless, penniless, and hopeless. My daughter, who was a senior at the time, had to move in with her father.

"Fight" was the word that I kept hearing. "Fight! Fight! Fight!" It resonated so deeply within me that it physically hurt. One night after my usual tirade with God (yes, I said tirade), I sat Indian style in the middle of the floor totally out of breath from screaming. And there it was. The realization that the woman I once knew was gone. I did not know this person that was screaming at God. I was not me. I was not acting like a woman who knew God at all. I did not have an address, a phone number, or anything of value to my name. The classy diva doll had turned into a rag doll with no purpose for being here, at least that is what I thought. Little did I know, I was silently and unconsciously fighting my way back on the inside. Let me share with you what I mean.

Everything I owned was gone, everyone I thought I could count on was gone, and every Scripture I knew I threw at God with malice. But, out of all I just named, do you see what I see? I was now a totally empty vessel; and, even though I did not pray an "Our Father" kind of prayer, I was still talking to God, everyday all day. He was wrapping me up in every Scripture I was shooting at Him. While sitting on that cold floor, I began to see myself right where I was—I was not me but it was me. I felt a warm sensation that penetrated my head and worked its way through my entire body as if I was being filled with something. I couldn't and didn't want to move. As the sensation consumed me, the words that left my lips were, "You can do this, you are not alone, and I have something for you to do so FIGHT!" As I laid down on the floor, a soft sweet whisper said, "If you FIGHT, the devil can't win."

It was the first time in months that I had smiled. Still in a weak state, I stood up, mentally brushed myself off, and made a much-needed concrete decision to FIGHT! The journey back to me was not easy, but God never left me. Through every obstacle and roadblock, He was there. What I learned was that God is not a vending machine or a magician. He can change or remove things at will; however, what would we learn from that? He is not a mean God. He does not watch you suffer and He was not the one who caused the home invasion; but, He is the one who kept me safe. He did not allow them to take my life. He kept me sane and He allowed me to share this story with you and many others to show that He never abandoned me, and He won't abandon you. There is a blessing and a lesson in all of this. And so it is written:

"And we know that all things work together for good to them that love God, to them who are the called according to His purpose."
—Romans 8:28 (KJV)

I am living proof that you can go through the fire and not smell like smoke. God was and is always there. In due season, all things have worked and will continue to work for my good. I am now back in school working toward my nurse practitioner MSN degree, I reinstated my current nursing license, and I am working in a hospice facility where God has used me to do some amazing things. He has given me back almost everything I have lost and I know the rest is coming.

"God will never leave you empty. He will replace everything you lost. If He asks you to put something down, it's because He wants you to pick something up!"—Frankie John

SOUL REFLECTION:
I now see God in a whole new light, and I humble myself daily whenever I think I am doing this life thing on my own. I know now what my calling is—that thing He spared my life for—and as long as I FIGHT, the devil can't and won't win!

Forgiveness

LASHONDA DAVISON

"And be ye kind one to another, tenderhearted, forgiving one another, even as God for Christ's sake hath forgiven you."

—Ephesians 4:32

My name is LaShonda, and I always start off by saying, "I hope all is well with you and your family!" when I'm addressing someone. I feel as if this is the polite thing to say to people. Wouldn't you agree? I wear many hats on different days or you can say I have several roles in this thing we call life. My first role is a child of God, without Him I am nothing. I am a mother of two beautiful, intelligent human beings, and I'm an advocate and activist for children's education. I am also an event planner and a politician. I am also engaged to an amazing man who I love dearly! That's just a little bit of who I am. I have a busy life, as we all do; but, I make sure that I make time for me. If I don't, I won't be able to help others. You always want to set some time aside for yourself. I thought I would just add that into my intro.

I want to talk about forgiveness. I know that's a touchy subject, but hey, here goes. What does forgiveness mean?

Well, let's see. Forgiveness is the action or process of forgiving or being forgiven. Forgiving someone is the hardest thing in the world to do, right? Especially if it's someone who is close to you. You love them so much and you know deep down they would never ever do anything to hurt you. So you think! Like, why would the person or people you love or care about hurt you? Well, people hurt people especially if they have been hurt. I know off-hand that forgiveness is not an easy road to go down. I have been hurt by several people in my life. This one I am about to talk about hurt the worst. I was married to my kids' father for 10 years. I can tell you I loved that man more than anything in this world. Sometimes I look back and say, "I think I loved him more than I loved myself." I met him when I was in college. It was the end of my freshman year. I will never forget. I was walking into the building where he worked, he stopped me, and the first words out my mouth were, "I have a boyfriend," and I kept walking. I finished whatever I was doing, and as I was walking back to my car he stopped me again. So, I thought, "He's one of those guys who is persistent." What happens next gets my attention. Mind you, I really was in a relationship at the time. We talked briefly, and he gave me his number. He said, "No pressure. Whenever you need to talk." Lol. Long story short, I left the state where I met him shortly after that to attend another school and he came to see me. We hung out for a while; then, the next thing I knew, I was back in that state a few months later and I was engaged to him.

Needless to say, that man was a great closer. We didn't have a wedding because I decided that it was too much stress planning one. So, we went to the good ole courthouse on his lunch break. How's that for a wedding! I tell people if you want to do the courthouse and cut out the stress, go for it. So now we are married and life is grand. I thought, "The man I married has no baggage and is the love of my life." Well, here comes something he didn't tell me about even though I asked him. Can you guess what it is? Yes, you guessed right... a child. A whole child. I said to him, "But wait, Buddy, what do you mean you have a child? I asked you if you had kids when we were getting to know each other. You said no." Of course, I was furious; but, what could I do? We were already married. I know some of you are saying, "You could have gotten an annulment." But, I was young and not even thinking about that. Plus, when I got married, I had every intention on being like my great-grandparents who helped raised me. Before my great-grandfather (aka: my daddy) passed, him and my great-grandmother (aka: mommy) were married for over 50 years. You know that's a blessing and so very hard to see nowadays. But, back to my ex! We had a long, and I mean long, talk about his child that magically appeared. I forgave him. We went about our lives, but I kept getting this feeling in my stomach. I never could put my finger on it though, so I ignored it. Well, one day guess what. I can't remember where we were, but he told me he had another child on the way. Yes, I said it. You don't have to reread what I said. Another one, but it was still in its mommy's womb. I asked him, "How?" He said, "It happened before we got married." I said, "That means you were sleeping around with her while we were dating. Go figure!"

    Once again, we had another long, drawn out conversation. We all know that I forgave him again. Mind you, all of this is happening within less than a year of our marriage. So now I'm this young woman with two step kids. I wasn't working because he didn't want me to work. Before we got married, I was a makeup artist living in Atlanta. The company I was working for wanted me to move to Chicago at that time. Of course, once we got married, I had to talk to him about it. He didn't want to move. Why? He used the excuse of the crime being too bad. But really, he just didn't want to.

After everything with the babies, time went on and we were happy because I forgave him. I told him, "Please, just be honest with me from here on out about everything." He agreed, and we went on about our wonderful life. Seeing as though I didn't work, it was only right that I kept the house clean, cooked, and made sure the bills were paid. Oh, let me not forget that I made sure my man was happy. His job was very demanding, so I wanted to make sure he was happy and that his dinner was ready for him when he came home. A lot of times, he didn't come straight home though. He would go hang out with his friends or co-workers and stay out very late. When he finally did come home, he would be drunk. So, I had to take care of him and sober him up. He wasn't always a very nice man during those times. But, I kept going like nothing was happening and no one ever knew. One day, I wasn't feeling like myself and my mind said, "Go grab a pregnancy test," so I did. I took it but I didn't believe it; so, I went back and bought three more tests. They all came back positive. I was so excited! I couldn't believe I was going to be a mom. That was the best news I ever had. I couldn't wait to tell him. I called him at work and said, "Hey, we are pregnant." When I told him, he didn't sound too excited.

Fast forward throughout my pregnancy and he continued to drink and drink and not come home. Don't get me wrong, our marriage was not all bad. We had some good times. I mean, I was married to him for ten years.

In the midst of all this, he was cheating. Yes, while I was pregnant with our baby. You know that gut feeling we as women get? (I can only speak for women because I am one.) I had that feeling. So what did I do? I started checking. Yes, looking at his call log, listening to his voicemails, checking his text messages, his emails, and his work voice mail. I knew that he wouldn't use any hard passwords, so I figured it out. That's how I got access to everything. And, get this. He even had numbers in his pockets. When I asked about them, he said they were for whoever he went out with that night. Mind you, that person was married as well. By now, I'm sure you are saying that I am crazy for putting up with all this. What I didn't mention earlier was that he was ten years older than me. But that didn't matter to me. I loved him because he honestly treated me good besides all that foolery. During this time, I gave birth to a beautiful, ten-pound baby girl a month early. It was a blessing that there were no complications and she was healthy.

Fast forward, we continued our lives with a new baby which now makes me a stay at home mom. I was still doing my wifely duties while he took care of home. He moved us into a bigger house, bought me a nice big car, and I shopped for us and the house. I guess he thought all that would take away the pain I was living with from knowing that he was still cheating. But, never would he admit to it. He would go out of town with his brothers and cousins, but he would never take me and our daughter. I played it off like I was okay; but, I got fed up and confronted him about it. He still wouldn't admit to it. I loved him, so I stayed and continued to act like everything was good. I mean, what do you do when he's taking care of you and your baby? I was young and thought I was on top of the world. All who knew us saw a good-looking family who loved one another and was doing well for themselves.

One day, we get into a big argument and he tells me all the women he has been with mean nothing to him. So, I ask, "Why do it then? Am I not enough?" He said yes, I was. I was everything and more. He just didn't know why he was doing what he was doing. I asked him, "So why did you marry me if you were going to cheat?" His response was, "I didn't want anyone else to have you." Wow! I didn't know what to say to that. I suggested that we go to counseling and of course that was a big no no. But, I kept asking and he finally decided to go. We went a few times, but it didn't work. It seemed to make things worse. At that point, I felt like I was just staying for the kids. Oh yeah, I had a bouncing baby boy amid the rest of the drama. I carried him for seven months. He weighed 6 pounds, 12 ounces. If you see him now you wouldn't be able to tell he was an early arrival. I tell him he just couldn't wait to meet his mommy. Let me say this, you never want to stay in a relationship for the kids' sake. You will be so miserable.

The straw that broke the camel's back was when he was working out of town for mother's day weekend. When he got off, he said he had a headache so he was going to go to bed and turn his phone off. I decided to call his hotel and check on him. Well, they said he checked out. How did I feel about that? Not happy at all. The next morning, I called his phone to check his voicemail and there was a message from a female saying how she had a wonderful time and thanks for flying her to where he was. Needless to say, that was it. I was done. I was beyond angry with him and over him. To me, there was no saving our marriage. He left, took everything with him, and left me with nothing. I had to move into an apartment with my babies and find a job.

How do you forgive someone who has done all of that to you? I was angry and didn't even want him seeing his kids. I loved that man so much and he did that to me. It took me years before I could even look at him. I asked God, "Why me?" I never understood that the mess he was taking me through was going to be my message or that all the tests were my testimonies. I have felt the pain that you are going through, and one piece of advice I can give is that it's going to be okay. You will make it out of it. But, don't do it alone. Talk to a close friend or family member you can trust. Scream or even cry if you have to. It's okay! I promise. Please don't forget to pray because without God you can't make it. I know it was my God and my babies that kept me going. Don't keep that anger balled up inside, it's not healthy.

Now, don't get me wrong, me forgiving him didn't happen overnight. It took a long time. But, when I started praying for him and getting over the anger, I finally forgave him. Now we co-parent and it's so much easier on all of us. Like I stated earlier, forgiveness is not easy at all. It takes time and prayer. I'm going to leave you with this verse from one of my favorite songs, the "Song of Intercession": "The change I want to see must first begin in me."

SOUL REFLECTION:
Be the change you want and don't walk around hurt. Be blessed my loves!

Trusting God Through the Process

LAVERNE M. PERLIE

*"Trust in and rely confidently on the LORD with all your heart
And do not rely on your own insight or understanding."*

—Proverbs 3:5 (AMP)

Excuse me, can I talk with you for a moment? I promise, I will not take up too much of your time. I've got something to talk about. How are you today? I'm LaVerne. What I'm about to share with you is a reflection from the depths of my soul, and it's for your ears only. There is something that God wants you to know. I'm sure you're eager to find out exactly what it is. It's Soul Talk for real, from me to you. I'm talking about trusting God through your process.

    I've experienced some situations in life that diminished my inner glow. Devastation, shock, disappointment, and pain have taken me places I just did not want to go nor do I ever want to return to. One consistent circumstance that troubled me for years involved sustaining a viable pregnancy. I'm a wife and a mother of two children; however, I've experienced multiple mixed type miscarriages. Yes! You heard me, mixed type. I've had two tubal pregnancies. One which ruptured and caused me to almost die from internal bleeding, and the other, a set of twins at nine weeks. I also had a stillborn at six months, and miscarriages at both four and eight weeks.

I tell you the truth, this was the most painful time in my life. It seemed as if everywhere I went, someone else was pregnant or announcing a new pregnancy, having a baby shower, or decorating a room and sharing their excitement. I must admit, there were days I smiled at others' happiness; but, on the other hand, I was mad as I don't know what concerning my misfortune. I questioned God. I said, "I'm married now. How come I can't keep these babies?" People meant well, but they would say, "Honey, God will not put more on you than you can bear. Accept His will that you were not meant to have those children." Or, "Sweetheart. God blessed you with one, be grateful!" I wanted to lay hands suddenly (not holy hands either) and lift them up high after hearing comments like that. But, I repented for my thoughts.

The stillborn was a boy; my husband and I were waiting for a son. I clearly remembered going to my OB/GYN's office and waiting to have his heartbeat checked. I didn't feel as much movement as I had previously, so I asked to come in. I can still see the beads of sweat on the obstetrician's forehead as he kept moving the Doppler over my large abdomen to check for a heartbeat. Then, the monitor showed a flatline and there was dead silence. Tearfully he said, "I'm sorry, Mrs. Perlie, but your baby has expired." I was six months pregnant and devastated.

Two months before finding out about this pregnancy, I dreamt that I delivered a child prematurely. I was in an operating room, it was cold, and I was presented a tiny baby wrapped in layers of small blankets. I said to the doctor in the dream (who happened to be a local news anchor in my hometown), "This can't be my baby because it's not time yet." That same night after awakening from the dream, I saw my husband sitting on the edge of the bed holding his head in his hands. I asked him what was going on. He said nothing. Then I told him what I dreamt.

Two years later, my husband revealed that that same night, he dreamt that he saw the baby in my womb choking on its umbilical cord. I stayed angry for a long time. I was too fearful to even attempt trying to get pregnant. I was so doubtful that a positive outcome would ever come my way again. I shut down, cut off friendships, family, and I just wanted to be alone. It was during this time that the enemy of my soul would whisper to me, "You aren't ever going to have any more children!"

The Bondage of Despair

Following that fetal death, I was a wreck. This was number four of my attempts to carry a child full term. In my withdrawn state, I felt many days like an empty shell. I was so taken aback by it all. I had lost my soul glow and was tied to the bondage of despair, doubt, and depression. I knew I had to leave this place, but I just couldn't seem to let go. If I didn't break away from these chains, I would self-destruct from the feelings of agonizing defeat, frustration, and worthlessness.

Two years later, I went to a prayer shut-in service. I had felt peace by joining other women in prayer monthly, but this service was different. A woman prayed for me and following the prayer she said, "The Lord said before this year ends, you will give birth to a male child, and you will not lose this child. God says He is going to carry him." I thanked her as I cried, cried, cried, and cried some more. Part of me truly wanted to accept what she said as truth and see this revelation come to pass, but I also wondered, "What if....?" My head began to fill with doubt and before you know it, fear had gripped and paralyzed me. In that second, I didn't want to think about another birth that ended up with me being discharged with my baby's belongings—undershirt, bracelet, footprints, and hat—in a box, while watching other mothers carry their babies in the car seat. I decided I was just too fearful and doubtful, and I would make an appointment for sterilization. I told my husband my concerns. He was fine with us having the one child and didn't wish to see me hurting any more.

Within two weeks, I scheduled my routine examination. During my visit, I told the nurse practitioner my plan. She said, "I'd like for you to have bloodwork done before we schedule any surgery, including a pregnancy test." I laughed to myself and said to her, "You don't have to worry about that, it's never going to happen again." Four days later, she called to inform me that I would not be able to have a tubal ligation performed because I was already eight weeks pregnant. As I hung up the phone, I sat in shock and cried. I was scared, doubtful, and tormented by the outcomes of the former pregnancies.

Fighting for My Freedom

Have you ever had to fight for your freedom? If not, I need you to hear me and hear me clearly. This is Soul Talk for real. God has given us the ability to fight or flee a situation based upon the release of specific chemicals in our body in response to an event, which produces a threat. Mind you, the enemy does not want you to learn how to defend yourself from any attack that comes your way. Therefore, I learned how to execute the power of prayer as my weapon of mass destruction to defend myself against the schemes of the enemy of my soul.

During the first trimester, I was tormented by dreams of miscarriage. I dreamt that I was in an operating room in stirrups. It was cold, but this time I started to see blood; large amounts were filling up the room. A voice coming from the loud speaker on the left side of the room shouted, "Stat, hysterectomy now!" It was so loud, and it got louder and louder. Staff were moving fast in the operating room. Then, another voice louder than the voice to my left shouted, "Cancel every satanic resolution over your life now!" It was a battle of the voices; both were loud and strong. But, with every declaration from the voice on the right speaking against what was happening, the power of the left sided voice was being diminished and over powered; so, eventually it ceased. The dream ended with a baby in a pair of large Caucasian hands, then the blood began to dry up and clear out from the room.

I awakened shaken and trembling. I got out of the bed, paced the floor, and sat back down trying to calm down. I prayed, "Lord God, I need you. Help us. I need to see the truth of Your revelatory Word. I believe you are the God who has the power to give and take life. I'm asking you to give me this life and not allow me to endure a miscarriage again. I trust You, and I will not doubt You because I believe Your Word is true. Instantly, the baby began to relax, and my heart rate slowed down. I was in bondage to fear and needed a release. I knew it was going to be a relentless fight.

This was the beginning of my fight for freedom.

Joy Unspeakable Joy

Before that night, I had hidden my pregnancy. I was close to five months before people began to ask if I was pregnant. I realized after that night if I was going to really trust God, I should not have any reason to be scared because my blessing was on the way. First, Proverbs 3:5 informs us that we are to "Trust in the Lord with all of our heart and not lean to our own understanding." To that end, you can't soulfully speak of trusting in God and doubt him by living in fear. Fear is a paralytic with magnetic attraction and suction cups. It takes everything you have in you, makes all lies appear realistic, and transfers your thoughts into a wilderness of assumptions, accusations, and false hope. Second, fear causes you to make poor decisions. Continued without intervention, fear will cause you to self-destruct and miss your opportunity for blessings. Third, fear is not supported in Scripture. 2 Timothy 1:7 says, "For God has not given us the spirit of fear, but of power, love, and a sound mind." Fear makes things seem impossible all of the time, and weakens you;

however, Philippians 4:14 says, "I can do all things through Christ that strengthens me." Therefore, I had to learn to trust God with everything in me, because in order to break away and remain free, I needed to draw closer to Him in prayer. I received strength. My prayer strategy changed. I started praying more specifically and fervently about the outcome of the pregnancy. I praised God for the blessing of a healthy, living child. I read the Bible to my unborn child. I began to purchase maternity garments and gather ideas for the child's room. I stopped begging God and believed Him!

The night before I went to my 24-week appointment, I had another dream. It was dark this time. Only voices were heard. I heard a voice on the left side say to me, "You are not going to hear a heartbeat." Then I heard another voice on the right declare, "God is going to make you laugh!" Then, the dream ended. When I awakened, the baby was moving ferociously as if fighting against a force trying to snatch him from the encapsulated domain of my womb. I anointed my belly, laid hands on my unborn child, prayed and said, "I get to hear you today." When we got to the appointment, the same obstetrician who pronounced our other son deceased was on duty. He stuttered as he shook my hand and reintroduced himself. I'm sure he remembered me, but we greeted as strangers. As he placed the cold gel on my belly and started moving it to find the baby's heartbeat, suddenly there was a loud kick and the pulsating sound of a strong heartbeat. I laughed uncontrollably for 10 minutes. The staff was puzzled and asked my husband, "Why is she laughing?" He said, "She is full of joy unspeakable joy!"

Divine Intervention

At 28 weeks I was put on bed rest due to an elevated blood pressure reading. This continued up until 32 weeks. During my 34-week appointment, I had gained over 60 pounds and my kidney function was abnormal. My blood pressure was 190/110; therefore, I had to be induced and was diagnosed with preeclampsia. During labor, I got a call from the same woman who prophesied the delivery of the child at the shut-in prayer service. She said, "I'm going to pray with you. I need to have my husband pray for your husband." We all prayed; then, I started having intense pain, and I felt lighted-headed and cold. I could not hear the baby's heartbeat any more. My husband and the baby's godmother were praying.

Faith in Action

The staff moved expeditiously. They checked the machines, administered IV medications, frequently checked my vital signs, and were trying to get the heartbeat to return. I felt like I was leaving this earth. Then, just like that, his heartbeat was captured. I smiled through the oxygen and facemask. An obstetrician I was not familiar with came into the room. He said he worked on the team with my doctor and he needed to check me. He examined me and said that I was ready, and he asked me to push. With my eyes closed, I started to push. The pain was so intense, I wasn't sure I could follow any directions. However, I was pushing past my fear, pushing past resistance, pushing past doubt, and I was about to give birth to my promise! After push number five, I was told to open my eyes. I saw a small, beautiful baby boy (who looked very much like his brother who had passed) in these large Caucasian hands... just like the dream. The next day, the woman from the shut-in called and told me that God told her to pray and ward off death. She said God had placed a large, white angel outside of my room with a sickle in his hand.

SOUL REFLECTION:

I encourage you to trust God and thank Him for everything in advance. I learned to activate my faith in the midst of adversity, uncertainty, and impossibility. I exchanged doubt for confidence, panic for praise, and sorrow for joy. God never said life would be a bed of roses, but He promises never to leave us. My baby is now 14 years old and all is well. Trust God in the process.

My Truth but God's Plan

KATHERINE ROMAR

We do this by keeping our eyes on Jesus, the champion who initiates and perfects our faith. Because of the joy awaiting him, he endured the cross, disregarding its shame. Now he is seated in the place of honor beside God's throne."

—Hebrews 12:2 (NLT)

Today, I sit thanking God for His grace and mercy! At one point, I felt my life was meaningless and desired to end it all. But God! I wasn't a mistake. God knew what He was doing. In accordance to Jeremiah 29:11 (MSG), "I know what I'm doing. I have it all planned out—plans to take care of you, not abandon you, plans to give you the future you hope for."

Raised in a small town located in Georgia, my mother did her best to provide for my siblings and me. We lived in low-income housing known as Roanoke Homes. My mother's income was not enough to ensure shelter, food, and clothing was available. So, we received state aid and food stamps.

I didn't wear the latest fashion, but I was always clean, fed, and had a warm place to lay my head. I wore handmade clothing and items that were considered outdated. The funny thing was that my siblings and I have never thought we were poverty-stricken. Again, but God!

My mother was no saint. She was married, never divorced, but separated with many lovers. My eldest brother was her husband's son, but the rest of us had different fathers. Again, we didn't allow any of this to deter her vision for us. My mother was determined to see all of us succeed where she failed. But, one by one, even though she never voiced her disappointment, my siblings and I did fail.

I found out I was pregnant my senior year of high school. I thought I was in love. After years of dating, I realized that it was lust. He and I were heading in different directions in life. I desired to see the world, and he was content with drinking and emulating his parents. I placed our daughter ahead of my dreams and visions. I worked and studied hard to obtain my high school diploma.

Upon graduation, I found myself still living in my mother's home with her assisting as much as possible. I was determined to make my mother proud of me. I attempted to go to the technical school, but my heart was not in it. I quit that and started to work at a local factory, but the noise was overwhelming. I desired more and decided to leave that job as well.

Life for me was not working. I was failing fast. I was a young mother who allowed my surroundings to kill my dreams. I went from being a creative writer in high school to a young mother attempting to provide for her child. I could not find my path. I ran from one bad relationship to another.

I found myself pregnant with my second child. The father to be was a low-grade drug dealer who was too immature to care for or provide for my child and me. I knew this, but I blindly held on to him and his deceptive lies. I worked hard but couldn't get ahead. Slowly, I saw myself repeating the sins of my mother. But I could not blame her. They were all my decisions. But, God's plans overrode mine!

At five months, I discovered I had syphilis. As I sat in the doctor's office, I was embarrassed, and I felt abandoned. My child's father was in jail and I couldn't speak with him. The doctor administered the prescribed shots of penicillin. I went home defeated and heartbroken. In my embarrassment, I did not tell a soul. That night, I cried, and wrote a letter to my so-called boyfriend.

Before I could finish the letter, I felt pressure in my abdomen and ran to the bathroom. Unbeknownst to me, I was in the beginning stage of miscarrying. As I sat on the toilet, I felt what I thought was a bowel movement. I was very light-headed and was losing blood and consciousness. I yelled for help, and my little sister ran to get someone.

My brother's girlfriend came and called for an ambulance. It was as if I was in a barrel. I couldn't respond nor move on my own. It seemed as if I was losing control of my own body. I heard the emergency technician tell the hospital that I needed blood and was losing color. At the hospital, I couldn't remember how to sign my name. I remember placing an x on the paperwork. I permitted them to give me blood, incinerate my fetus, and perform dilation and curettage.

I woke up in a hospital room with my mother looking at me with tears in her eyes. She told me about my blood transfusions and how close to death I had come. She shared with me that I was very pale and very incoherent when she arrived. I cried but was still afraid to share the truth with her. If she knew, we never discussed it. That afternoon, my baby's other grandmother came to visit, and she told me that the miscarriage was a blessing because I needed to get far away from her child. She shared with me that her son would not be suitable for my daughter and me. After an hour or so, his mother departed, and I sat alone in the hospital room. I mourned my son and cried softly to myself until sleep took over. A day or two later, I was discharged.

At home, I pretended to be fine, but I was depressed. My world was my child and work. I did nothing else. I was afraid to move forward. I knew I had to do better, but I didn't know the proper steps to take. I decided to live by clubbing and hanging out with friends. These particular friends smoked pot. One night, I decided I wanted to be high and numb my feelings; but, the pot hurt me. Instead of feeling high, I felt nauseated and my head began to throb. I left my friends and told my mom who became outraged. I woke the next morning feeling somewhat better, and decided to do it again. The second time was worse than the first! I was in the club and it seemed as if the music was exploding in my brain. I left the club feeling desperate and began walking home. I wanted to run but I had nowhere to go.

But God had a plan for me that exceeded my vision and understanding. As I walked home, the Holy Spirit brought back to my memory an earlier encounter with these older women at this church one summer when I went to Atlanta and stayed with my cousins who were deeply religious. It was their revival time, and of course, they had church from Tuesday to Sunday. Personally, I had no intimacy with

God nor understanding of how He provided for me. In one service (I remembered it like it was yesterday), my cousin led me up to the altar. At the platform, these older women surrounded me as they prayed both in unknown tongues and using God's Word. Due to my ignorance, fear set in and I stood only half listening. I now know that the words they spoke were prophetic. It took me years to comprehend it all, and I ran far away from religious places and people. I swore off the church and decided the believers were crazy.

Shortly after my walk home, I decided to call my local United States Army recruiter. I joined the Army and left my daughter two days before her second birthday. Basic Training was terrible, but I endured. My first duty station was in South Korea. I survived over 20 years of service and traveled to many other countries.

Even in that, I was not content. Promotions didn't come. I worked hard, but in my spirit, I couldn't find joy. I experienced animosity, sexual harassment, and depression. However, I am thankful for every situation, circumstance, storm, and tribulation, as each one pressed me into the arms of my first love.

I went through a lot of heartaches. Some were self-imposed and some were inflicted by others whom I allowed into my inner circle. I was romantic and defined love strictly by emotions and feelings. I felt as if a man was supposed to end all sorrows and rescue me from my dungeon. I gave my whole heart time after time but ended up broken.

I married my first husband within months of meeting him. I dealt with him being unfaithful. I foolishly believed all his lies. He controlled me, and I sat idly by as he ran around with an ex-girlfriend who eventually gave birth to their child. I still held on thinking I could change him. God again had His hand on my life and saved me from taking my ex's life. Once he got tired of playing house, he left me penniless, without a car, and very bitter. Eventually, I was drawn back into God's loving arms.

I have since been married, divorced, and married again. I am the wife of a very loving and caring man. We have had our share of ups and downs and broken each other's hearts, but we refuse to let go. God's love prevails. I am the mother of four beautiful daughters and a grandmother to my first grand-sugar.

Today, I am fifty years young. I sabotaged my own life for years. I wallowed in self-pity. I ran from church to church and moved from country to country. I even hurt my family with my foolishness. My husband and I have both committed adultery on numerous occasions. Through it all, I have established an intimacy with God. I am learning to forgive as well as see my husband as God sees him. I no longer try to fix him.

One day, my husband, Kirk, told me I had a victim mentality. Angry, I decided divorce was the best course of action. I rationalized, but through prayer and meditation, my truth of victimization outweighed my denial. I had to press in through prayer and fasting. As I developed my intimacy with God, I also linked up with a counselor who helped me uncloud my judgment of the duties of my husband.

I would like to end my chapter confirming that Kirk and I are living our fairy tale, but that would be a lie. The truth is we are taking it day by day. Some days are better than others, but I refuse to give up on my marriage. I have begun to see another counselor. I know that life presents issues, but my established trust in my God shall be evident as I continue with my process.

I have taken ownership for destroying my marriage and causing my daughters to experience anxieties. My Father, God, knew all this would occur. It was all in His plan to pull me into His loving arms. I have spoken with my daughters, and they have forgiven me. We are on the road to repairing our relationships. I have shared more of my truth with them, and through our conversations we are learning to speak to and listen to each other, lessening the anger and tears. I intend to prevent them from repeating my sins. I thank God for His Holy Spirit's guidance, and for teaching me humility and how to forgive and seek forgiveness.

As for my husband and I, I have offered him as much of my truth as he will allow. For now, I continue to see my counselor and have decided to take it day by day. My trust is in God, and whatever He has planned for our marriage shall be. Until He, through His Holy Spirit, reveals otherwise, I shall continue to fight my good fight of faith with nothing but expectancy and patience. I trust now that my husband's love for me is real and our vows shall endure until the end of time.

God's plan shall unfold with each blessed day. I do trust Him and know that Jesus is the Author and Finisher of my faith (Hebrews 12:2). I made my choice to submit to God and walk in obedience to His call. I pray that by sharing my story, I encourage you to first and foremost develop an intimate relationship with our Creator and Father, God. Doing so will lessen the blows that will come to keep you from obtaining all of God's promises and living eternally with Him.

With each blessed day, life becomes easier to endure. The keys that I have found to work for me are simple.

Key 1: Stay focused on God. Philippians 3:15-16 tells us to tap into the mind of Christ through submission to our indwelling Holy Spirit's teaching of our Father God's Truth. The more time we spend in His presence and meditate on His Word, it will produce like-mindedness; and like Jesus, our agenda will be God's.

Key 2: Trust must be in God. Romans 15:13 tells us to trust God through all, in all, and with all. Through His Holy Spirit's teaching and guidance comes His joy and peace. As His son or daughter, you will be filled with high expectation and blessed assurance.

Key 3: Discover your purpose. Ephesians 2:8-10 tells us that as believers all credit belongs to our Father, God. We must walk in obedience as His Holy Spirit leads and guides us to our predestined purpose within the body of Christ.

Key 4: Endure through all. 2 Corinthians 1:3-5 tells us that as believers we must rely wholly on God's Holy Spirit to be (as He is called) our Comforter. As He comforts us, those watching shall recognize our strength and peace that surpasses all understanding. Then, in turn, we can genuinely help others as we share the good news of our Father God's love, mercy, and grace.

SOUL REFLECTION:
There are so many guidelines and promises found in our book of instructions, the Bible. I am learning to take life one day at a time and rely on God. His Word is real, and loneliness shall evade us all if only we release people and look to the hills to see our Helper! Our God is omnipotent, omniscient, and omnipresent. Answer His call.

The Awakening

DIONNE SELBY

"Faith without works is dead."

—James 2:26 (KJV)

I have the gift and the curse of striving for perfection. As a life coach, I help people find their passion, accomplish their goals, and become their best self. I was raised in the church; however, I will openly admit that I acknowledged who God was in my life, but I had no real relationship with Him. It took a few trials and tests to get to where I am today. "Faith without works is dead" is one of my favorite Scriptures and it helped to teach me a couple of lessons. You hear that Scripture and unless you've really been through some challenging times in life, you don't really know what it means. But as soon as life starts to hand you more lemons than you can bear, you start to feel and experience those words. So, let's break this down. "Faith" by definition is to have complete trust or confidence in someone or something or to have belief that is not based on proof. Then you have the second part of the Scripture, "without works." Sounds kind of awkward because it has "works" as a plural word right in the middle of a sentence. Lastly, the most powerful part to me of the entire Scripture is "is dead." You know why that is the most powerful part of the Scripture to me? Because the word dead is final. In the sentence, dead is referencing the actions of your faith.

I'm sure you've heard the importance of your actions speaking louder than your words. In this case, your actions must speak louder than your faith. This happens to be one of the biggest lessons I've learned so far in life. If you want things to happen, you will have to apply your works. There is no way around it. Well, at least I think most of us think so, especially control freaks such as myself. I also like to call myself a doer. You know, the kind of person that doesn't mind doing the work but wants complete control of how the work should be done. The kind of person that has the details in place, is used to planning the future, loves taking notes and asking questions, and still goes above and beyond to get things done. Sounds like a pretty awesome, over-achieving person who probably appears to do everything right. Right? That's exactly what I used to hear all the time as well. However, in hindsight, I had no clue as to the arrogant, inconsiderate, somewhat selfish, and controlling individual I was being, until God humbled me. That's where the real part comes in of that Scripture. I like to call it the hidden, life experience part, the "works." When this part hits you and you are humbled, everything you ever knew falls completely apart and you learn that you actually don't have complete control after all.

Have you ever gone through life thinking that you would have a checklist or that you could plan things out? I can't be alone in this way of thinking. Behave and be respectful in grade school. Weren't we taught that was the smart thing to do? Isn't that also how most of us are taught to act as responsible adults? Be focused, proactive, and intentionally ready for life. Fall in love, then comes the marriage, and after that the baby in the baby carriage, right? These are all the things we heard and were taught growing up. This is what becomes of our expectations of life. This is how it's supposed to play out. We get these instructions in our minds and we stick to them. We are supposed to have the best of friends, especially the ones we've invested the most time and feelings into. We make sacrifices for people and they are supposed to return the favors. We are taught that if we apply ourselves in college and in our careers, we are supposed to make the most money.

It doesn't seem possible that you could do everything right, and things still come out completely wrong. How is it that you can be a very good person, and still have terrible things happen? It doesn't seem fair. It almost seems personal. It's like, why would a person that is trying to do everything right and treat everyone right have to be wronged? Or why would you have to deal with any drama, chaos, or negativity? I know these are all questions we ask ourselves at some point. When these things happen, we feel angry, frustrated, and in some cases even depressed because we don't have the answers! We want to know why. We want to know what we could have done so poorly to deserve it, especially if we have tried to do the right things. Well, that's where these life lessons come in. I'd like to share these challenges that come into our lives to teach us to do the work.

If you're a planner and you are arrogantly going through life making decisions for yourself, you think you are in control. Sure, to some extent you have to be the writer of your own journey. You have to envision yourself as the driver of the car to get where you really want to be. However, the part we forget is that we don't have full control. There is a Higher Power. What if the Higher Power doesn't think you need to be in that relationship? What if the Higher Power doesn't think it's best for you to have that job? Maybe it's not the right timing for you to step out and pursue that business. What if there are some things you need to learn?

That's how I learned that the Scripture "faith without works" was not written just for fun and giggles. It was written with real meaning, real purpose. Real events will happen where you will have to apply this Scripture. For me, I guess I always heard the Scripture but hadn't really experienced anything life shattering to have to apply it to. Then, as I started to get older and took on challenges such as a stressful and demanding career in leadership, becoming a wife, and motherhood, I was far away from simply hanging with friends and wondering what party or weekend event to get into. Life got real. I literally had things happen where I screamed out for help. Friends that had always been a part of my life who said they would always be there, were nowhere to be found when I started to struggle. I experienced things in my marriage and as a mother that I don't want to share with my parents or family members due to shame or embarrassment. Or maybe you had that arrogant attitude where you never thought certain things could happen to you, but now you find yourself going through them. You literally call on God. You have no one else to turn to. That's why I love the Scripture so much because often we put some much trust and faith in other people that we forget all about God. I imagine God is like, "What about me? Have you forgotten that I am here for you to rely and focus on? Do you think about Me, do you remember that I still exist?"

    I truly believe there are no coincidences and that everything happens for a reason. What if those devastating situations were there to wake me up? To help me put my focus on my higher self, my Higher Power, and what really matters in life. What if I were to stop relying on other people and myself so much to get through this thing called life? When you do, you realize that's where that thing called a personal relationship with God comes in. You have to have faith in God. You have to practice letting go and give whatever it is that is challenging you or trying to defeat you to God. You have to know that every day is a personal journey and you are intentionally letting God guide your every thought and move. Just like you would do with your friends or close family members, you do the same with God. That's how beautiful the relationship becomes. The more you put your faith in God and make Him the focus of your life, the more you start to realize you are putting in the "works" as the Scripture suggests. You can have faith in life all you want; however, if you aren't applying the actual work, nothing will occur. Your faith is dead: expired, gone, and no longer alive. Once I started to realize this, I found that applying the works brought so much more life to the relationship I thought I once had.

    I thought that because of the way I was raised or because I acknowledged God, we had a relationship and I would be favored. Wrong! Life will certainly humble you back into the awareness of who is really in control and how a true relationship is supposed to operate. There are no words to describe the experience between you and God. It opens your eyes, your heart, and your mind to a new way of life. You begin to learn to love the process of being given blessings and challenges because you know they are sent for your good. Think back to the last challenge you had that really stirred you, and think about how you survived what you thought would kill you. Think about how much stronger or wiser you are from it. From that experience, you leveled up so much higher and have more insight to share with others. After your challenges, you understand that you have a responsibility and there is so much more to your being than the simple, petty things that may have distracted you before. You know you have purpose. You know that there are things you have to accomplish that your soul has yearned to do, and now like a child again, you have been given everything you need to be able to fly like a bird and reach your highest potential.

After gaining clarity of James 2:26 from my real-life experiences, I became fearless in my life. I found my life's passion through soul searching and discovering the power of putting works with my faith. I became fearless and much more aware about the journey of life. I gave my husband and any struggles or obstacles over to God. As a mother, I stopped being so hard on myself and instead learned to enjoy the journey. I practiced making mistakes and learning from them instead of holding myself to a secret agenda of perfection. I realized the Higher Power wanted me to be more and to do more.

Despite the calling on your life, you will still be tested. It's up to you to see if you will pass your tests. They will come and go, put know that if you are always putting in the work along with having faith, everything is working together for your greater good. Whatever those tests and trials were, they strengthened your faith and made you a force to be reckoned with. There is a sense of gratitude that comes from those challenging experiences. Gratitude in knowing there is an Energy supporting you when you fall and cheering you on like your best friend. You know there is a peace and calm that will always come after any storm. You know that where much of your life was dead it has now transitioned itself into being very alive. There has been an awakening inside of you. You are in tune with life's opportunities. You live life with excitement, joy, and optimism. You can't wait to try new things; you can't wait for new experiences. Where you were previously anxiously planning every moment of your life and thinking you can perfectly design events according to your liking, you are now instead aware that there may be a mess to clean up every now and then or some mistakes to correct. You can openly own being perfectly flawed in all aspects as you continue to grow and becoming your best self. You now know that faith without works is truly dead, and that fear and being in control was just a figment of your imagination.

SOUL REFLECTION:
God is within me. I would like to leave a legacy. I would not like to be famous, but I would like my work to be. I believe we all have a purpose, and mine is to inspire others.

I Knew It Was Time to JUMPP

DANA CAMPBELL

"May God himself, the God of peace, sanctify you through and through. May your whole spirit, soul and body be kept blameless at the coming of our Lord Jesus Christ. The one who calls you is faithful, and he will do it."
—1 Thessalonians 5:23-24 (NIV)

When you are in relationship with a friend, significant other, or spouse there is an inner spirit voice you hear but most often ignore. You must be in tune with this voice; the Holy Spirit. This voice will quite often speak loud and clear and may cause something to stir in your soul. This warning signal was given to us by God to make sure we stay on our path toward righteousness, to make sure nothing deters us from God's plan for our lives.

It is so important that you are on one accord with your spouse or significant other. There must be a level of respect, honesty, and vulnerability in order to form a bond of trust. Each person must be accessible—mind, body, and spirit. Since day one, my husband and I never seemed to be able to communicate on the same level; we never seemed to understand one another. There was always tension in the air. No matter what I did or said, nothing was truly satisfying to him. In hindsight, I realized a relationship that was supposed to be easy, was complicated. I believe there were instances when the voice of God was speaking to me; but, I was not familiar with His voice nor His Word. Years went by, and no matter how hard I tried to change the tone of my voice and the words I used, it seemed that my husband and I always spoke different languages. The conversation always seemed to end on a negative note. We walked away feeling wounded and unaccomplished. When facing a difficult circumstance with my husband I relied on "my" knowledge and "my" strength to develop a strategy to fix a problem or to communicate.

Journal Entry Reflections, 4/21/17:

Sometimes I feel sad and mad at the path my life has taken. I am not broken but I am bent because I knew we were not meant to be. I also didn't want to be a part of something that failed.

When you feel like you keep hitting a wall with your spouse, you may begin to think, "Why can't we understand one another?" A simple thought or suggestion seemed like a game of tug-of-war. I would often reflect on the difference in our upbringing and religious foundations. I even reflected on how we differed in disciplining our children. I did not have a positive image of what marriage should be. I did not have the opportunity to see two parents work together as a team exemplifying the fruits of the Spirit with one another. I had no idea what it meant to be evenly yoked. It became more and more evident that my husband and I were not evenly yoked in the spirit or in our patterns of thinking. Tired of subjecting our three children to the resentment, verbal disputes, and the growing tension between us, I had to make a life-changing decision. So, I decided to separate from my husband with the intent to file for divorce. I made my first JUMPP and moved into my own place with our children.

It wasn't until I separated from my husband that I reflected on my youth and realized that while growing up I didn't think much about having a family and getting married. It honestly never crossed my mind to get married. You may reflect on your past and wonder what happened growing up to make you who you are today. I want to take you back through my journey.

I believed I was an ordinary child growing up in a normal family, with a mom and dad that lived together and an older sister and younger brother. My parents had their challenges paying bills, but we always had a roof over our heads and food on the table. I aspired to go to college and participated in extracurricular activities. My upbringing did not show me a healthy picture of what marriage should be. I witnessed my parents making negative and demeaning comments to each other during my childhood. Most often, they were not a team making decisions as partners.

I remember giving my life to Christ Jesus at about the age of 12 during a summer visiting my grandma in South Carolina. During the following summer, my aunt gave me my first New King James Bible with my name on it. I thought this was such a special gift, but I did not understand the significance of the gift and the journey I was going to embark on. Fast forward, I went away to college. I formed friendships and relationships. I later remember rededicating my life to

God in my mid-twenties. I continued my relationship with God and with a man I call my first love. I would reach out to and rely on my boyfriend to fill the void I had but could not articulate. I was shy and introverted at the time and mostly desired and demanded his attention.

After later attending and completing graduate school and moving back to my hometown, my boyfriend and I remained in touch briefly, then it seemed that life took over. I began investing in myself and my career, and our relationship slowly became nonexistent. During this time, I stayed to myself and occasionally went out with close friends. In a year's time, 2007, a guy began to court me. I enjoyed the attention I received from him daily. In five months' time, we started a relationship. I was with a man who I believed loved me because he always wanted to spend time with me. We dated for about a year. Most of our activities consisted of us hanging with his friends.

In 2008, we had our first son. When I became pregnant, I put on my "big girl panties" and became a responsible mother. Indirectly, we talked about marriage. Since we were expecting a child together, we were influenced by my family to get married because it was "the right thing to do." During my pregnancy, I didn't feel honored as the mother of his first born; at times, I felt alone and isolated. When our son was six months old, we were married by a justice of the peace.

Several years and three children later, I still felt isolated and silently longed to be heard, respected, and understood. Notice I said three children. Yes, I became pregnant and decided to abort our last child after realizing I had no support from my husband. At that time, we were spiraling downhill.

After making the decision to have an abortion, I felt that I truly disappointed God. There were many times that I also felt invaluable, undesirable, unhappy, isolated, and embarrassed. I often asked myself, "Why doesn't he care about me or my feelings enough to put me and our marriage first?" "Why doesn't he understand where I am coming from?" Most importantly, "Why didn't he apologize for not being there during and after the abortion?"

Several months passed and several other events happened which further confirmed why it was time to JUMPP. I was surrounded by men and women of God. They taught and counseled me through the Word and always encouraged me to seek God before making any moves. After weeks of prayer and everything literally falling into place within one years' time, I heard God say, "It's time to GO!" I woke up one day after praying for weeks and talking to God day in and day out about what I should do. After waiting and listening for God's direction, I made arrangements to safely move out. This was the hardest decision I had ever made. But, in the previous two years, God had graced me with a job with a higher salary (I was financially stable), a brand-new car, and He allowed me to be approved for an apartment with one month's free rent. I was on the right path.

Journal Entry Reflection, 4/22/17:

I was at the thrift store in Lewisdale today. A young man with a lisp and a stutter complimented me on my Skechers and asked how comfy they were. Then he said I am going in the right direction. That was definitely a God moment.

You will have many times in life when God sends what I believe are His angels to give you encouragement and peace about the situations you are going through. One day, I gave myself permission to take some time out to enjoy one of my favorite pastimes. I had a rough week with work and my children seemed to be overwhelming me. I was second-guessing the decision I made to leave the heartache behind. That angel message made me feel more confident about the decision I made to separate from my husband and become a single mother with three children.

I am so grateful to God for His continuous lessons. For many years, I knew I needed to leave my marriage. I needed to leave the heartache and pain that I allowed to happen to me. I needed to have more self-love and self-compassion. For so long I was concerned about my children and how they would transition if I separated from my marriage. I recommend making sure you are safe from harm or danger. You know your situation better than anyone else. If you feel your spouse will be upset in any way, enlist support from a trusted friend, support group, or the police. In most states and counties, there is a domestic violence unit to contact for police escort or support. In my case, it was suggested by my spiritual counselor to have men in my church reach out to my spouse. I also had family help support my move, not to interfere but to be watchful.

I can tell you that children truly are resilient and are more keenly aware than we realize. Believe it or not, the children were more resilient than I was initially. There were some behavior concerns and rebellion, for that I do recommend counseling. Overall, in the past two years, our children have clearly verbalized their likes and dislikes, curiosities, and questions. I recommend being honest and truthful while respecting the innocence of your children; also respect the parent-child relationship. Most importantly, do not talk badly about the other parent to or in front of the child, this can be very hurtful. Lastly, do not stress about what your spouse says about you to or in front of your children. You cannot control the actions of others and your children will eventually recognize it as inappropriate. As painful as it may be, always pray positively for your children and spouse.

During my separation, I wrote the prayer below. I would also read John 15:5. It reminded me that I must stay connected to Christ. Without Him I cannot do anything. With Him I will prosper.

Journal Entry Prayer 4/23/17:

Please, Lord God, help me through this time of hurt and my lack of self-compassion. Disease, abortion, and divorce have all made me ashamed of who I am; yet, I understand they all have made me who I am.

"I am the vine; you are the branches. If you remain in me and I in you, then you will produce much fruit. Without me, you can't do anything."

—John 15:5 (CEB)

There comes a time in everyone's life when you must surrender it all to God, especially in those times when you feel like you are fighting a never-ending battle and you cannot win. I realized I needed to fully "let go and let God" when the writing was on the wall. It became clear that my husband and I were broken. God allowed me to see several actions and signs to let me know it was time to get ready to let go. God had given me signs and messages before, but He was very clear in announcing to me that it was time to move on and that that part of our lives could not be fixed.

I truly believe that God prepared me to be ready. One person and moment at a time, He placed special people in my life to counsel me through the Word of God, to give me strength, and to show me love. At the same time, He moved people out of my life. Some temporarily and others permanently. I know it was because He wants me to focus on Him and continue to grow and learn through lessons He provides. I have learned so much about myself and experienced several metaphorical, spiritual, and physical JUMPPs including skydiving, which was the most invigorating experience of my life. This journey is teaching me to get out of my own way and strive to show myself unconditional self-compassionate love.

If you are in a relationship with a significant other or a marriage and you know something isn't quite right, recognize that it's the Holy Spirit stirring something inside of you. Literally, stop what you are doing and be still. Be still! Let that Spirit touch you and talk to you (it may be a whisper or a loud tone). Simply receive what is being said, then say, "Amen." If you are trying to move past your situation, know that God sees and feels all you are dealing with. Surround yourself with people that will nurture you with the fruits of the Spirit and most importantly feed you with the Word of God. God will deliver on His promise to protect you from all hurt, harm, or danger.

Your journey is personal and uniquely designed for you. No person can dictate it. Trust, believe, and know that we all have a purpose. Most importantly, pray! Thank God for peace, joy, grace, and mercy. Thank God for keeping you. Thank God for forgiving you. Thank God for rescuing you. Invite Him to order your steps and bridle your tongue. Most importantly, ask God for greater discernment in your life.

Journal Entry Prayer, 7/30/17:

Lord, thank you for all you have given me. All you have birthed in me. All you have shown me. Thank you for all you had me go through to pull me closer to you. Amen.

> "God is within her, she will not fall."
>
> —Psalm 46:5

SOUL REFLECTION:

JUMPP

My JOURNEY became reality by UNDERSTANDING who I was in Christ. Then, the MANIFESTATION of His PURPOSE became my PASSION.

Stop Cheering and Get in the Game!

ANGELA T. KINNEL

"We love because he first loved us."

—1 John 4:19 (NIV)

Growing up in my hometown of Dawson, Georgia, was a lot of fun. Back then, we actively played games like kickball, hide-and-seek, and anything else we could think of. As kids, we spent a lot of time playing in a big open space behind my grandmother's house on Cherry Street. On this particular day, all the kids in the neighborhood decided to play a game of kickball. I was the youngest in the group. I had a lot of cousins in that neighborhood, so I knew I would be ok. My team and I were one out away from winning the game. We were in the outfield. So, while standing in my designated area, I started doing a cheer that I'd learned. I was near one of my big cousins. Her name was Tania and she was always nice to me. But on this day, she wasn't very nice at all. I'm standing there in la-la land cheering and I suddenly hear her yelling at me. Tania looked at me and said, "Meka," (my nickname) "stop cheering and get in the game!" I was crushed. My first reaction was to cry but I held it in. I didn't want them to call me a crybaby. My feelings were hurt but I figured that I'd go ahead and get in the game. Needless to say, once I became focused and paid attention to what was going on, I was the one who caught the ball in order to win the game.

For years, I never thought of that day until life began to happen and sent me into a deep four- year depression. At that point in my life, things seemed to be broken and stagnant. It began in 2003. I was working for a public gaming company that ironically paid low salaries, my college sweetheart decided to marry someone else, my grandmother transitioned to her heavenly home, one of my closest college friends ended our friendship without my knowledge, and I was spiritually empty. In addition to all of that, I fell down a flight of stairs and injured my back. I was out of work for a month. I felt like a functioning failure.

I prayed, but it was with doubt. I charge that to not knowing my real identity in Christ. When you don't understand and embrace who you truly are in Him, attacks like depression, emptiness, and low self-esteem come upon you. I gained a lot of weight and felt very unattractive. I left my corporate job and began working in the hotel industry. After being there for four months, my department was closed due to mismanagement of funds. It turned out that my boss embezzled thousands of dollars to support his crack habit. I moved on to a job in the airline industry and was placed on furlough six months later. I was at my lowest by then. One night, I went out on my balcony and surrendered to the Lord. I told Him to have His way with my life. I was tired of defeat. The next day, I was offered an interview for a position at a well-known university. It went well, and the department director recognized me from handling his account at the hotel. About two weeks later, I was offered the position. I was happy because I was finally utilizing my degrees. I had a good job, awesome benefits, and a nice office with an administrative assistant. However, I was still in that dark place inside. Even though I was depressed, I was always encouraging others to do this and that. Follow your dreams! But, I never thought about encouraging myself.

While working with the university, I had the opportunity to work with children. Through those experiences, I decided to become an educator in 2006. I began to pursue the credentials that I needed to teach in the state of Georgia. I went to a job fair and was hired on the spot. It's amazing how even at my lowest, the Lord was working things out for my good. I finally had a job that I loved, and I felt like I had purpose in life. Yet, I was still ignorant about my true identity. I began to talk to God more often and attended church regularly. The more time I spent with Him, the better I felt. After a week of living in my newly purchased house, I looked up at the ceiling and all the weight and emptiness I'd been feeling for so long left me. I took a deep breath and thanked God for delivering me from all of it. It was in that moment that I realized I'd stop cheering for everyone else and gotten in the game.

I truly believe that once you surrender your cares and your life to God, it opens the door to the grace, mercy, and favor that's on your life due to the finished work of Jesus Christ. To know God is to have a personal relationship with Him. Grace is free to take over when God is in the center of your triumphs and your chaos. Grace is God's undeserved, unmerited, and unearned favor.

Favor: Is it fair?

A few years ago, I went to my hometown to surprise my mother at church. It was around Christmas and she'd expressed how she wished that my brother and I would join her back home for worship. I got up early that Sunday morning and drove down to my hometown. My mother was pleasantly surprised, and I was happy to see her happy. After the service, I pulled out of the parking lot and blew out a tire. While waiting on help to replace my tire, an old acquaintance walked over to check on the situation. After greeting one another, he asked how things were going with me. I stated that I was doing well and happy to be home for Christmas. He stated, "Wow, you have a nice car and you own your own home. Man, favor ain't fair." I wasn't surprised at what he said. However, I was disturbed at how he said it. It didn't sound as if he was happy for me. I became offended. I started asking myself whether I deserved to have nice things and furthermore, what did he mean by "favor ain't fair?"

What is favor? I've read so many explanations. One definition said that favor means gaining approval, acceptance, or special benefits or blessings. Another definition said that favor was tangible evidence that a person has the approval of God. While those explanations could be deemed true, I decided to research the word myself. The origin of the word favor comes from the Latin word favere, which means show kindness to. Favor in Greek is charis (feminine noun). Charis means grace, favor, and kindness. Grace is referred to as a gift or blessing brought to man by Jesus Christ. That made me wonder if favor and grace were related. A Christian writer by the name of Bill Johnson stated in an article that "God's grace is His unmerited favor toward men through the blood of His Son. This unmerited favor includes not only being forgiven of sin but also receiving access to the very presence of God in the same way Jesus has access to Him." In testifying about Jesus, John stated in John 1:16 (AMP), "For out of His fullness (abundance) we have all received [all had a share and we were all supplied with] one grace after another and spiritual blessing upon spiritual blessing and even favor upon favor and gift [heaped] upon gift." I concluded that they are related because it seems that you can't talk about grace without mentioning favor. In Hebrew, favor means chen (masculine noun). Favor can be found throughout the Bible from Genesis to Revelations. Proverbs 8:35 (KJV) states, "For whoso findeth me findeth life, and shall obtain favour of the Lord." Jeremiah 29:11 talks about how God knows the plans He has for you. Plans for peace and to give you an unexpected end. That's chen!

Now that I knew where the favor came from and the Hebrew and Greek forms of the word, I was still unsatisfied. In order to truly understand why favor wasn't fair, I had to understand favor. I had to go a little deeper! I looked in the Merriam-Webster Collegiate Dictionary to see what favor meant. As a noun, favor is defined as friendly regard shown toward another especially by a superior; approving consideration or attention; partiality; a special privilege or right granted or conceded. As a verb, favor means to do a kindness for; to treat gently or carefully; to show partiality toward; prefer; to give support or confirmation to; to afford advantages for success to. The word partiality stood out to me, so I looked into what it meant. Partiality means the quality or state of being partial. Partial means markedly fond of someone or something. That made me think back to Jeremiah 29:11! God loves us so much that He released all of this extraordinary kindness on us and through us.

The question at hand still remains though, why is favor not fair? It seems to be available to all that believe so why is it not fair? I looked into the word fair and what it meant. The dictionary defined fair as marked by impartiality and honesty; free from self-interest, prejudice, or favoritism. Synonyms of fair included just, equitable, impartial, and unbiased; free from favor toward either or any side. Hold up! Wait a minute! Fair means free from favor? Well, that answers my question generally. Favor means partiality or to show partiality toward. But fair means free from favor, so favor really isn't fair!

While favor isn't fair, God is fair! What He does for one, He will do for another. How then does the Word of God back that up? I have 10 reasons why favor isn't fair, but God is:

1. God's favor brings supernatural events like increase and promotion. (Genesis 39:21)
2. God's favor brings one hundred-fold restoration of everything that the adversary has stolen from you. (Exodus 3:21)
3. God's favor brings joy in the presence of your enemies. (Exodus 11:3)

4. God's favor brings increase in your assets. (3 John 2)
5. God's favor brings great victories in the middle of great impossibilities. (Luke 1:37)
6. God's favor brings unexpected recognition from others. (Proverbs 3:4)
7. God's favor brings preferential treatment. (Esther 2:17)
8. God's favor brings petitions granted by ungodly people. (Esther 5:8)
9. God's favor allows rules and laws to be supernaturally changed and reversed for your advantage. (Esther 8:5)
10. God's favor allows victory in battles which you won't have to fight because God has already fought them for you. (Psalm 44:3)

Thank God for His unmerited favor!

When you stop cheering on the sidelines and get (participate) in your life, your confidence will develop, and your mindset will change. As believers, we must rest in the finished works of Jesus. Renewing your mind, confessing, and meditating on the Word activates what He has made available to us. We must never worry. Worry is a negative form of meditation. Right thinking produces right believing. Get a positive mindset! You must believe with all of your heart in God's love for you. He loves us with an everlasting love. Because of John 3:16 (KJV), we are free to love ourselves and others:

"For God so loved the world, that he gave his only begotten Son, that whosoever believeth in him should not perish, but have everlasting life."

SOUL REFLECTION:
We have operating in us the great, intense love that God used toward Jesus. We are the light of the world and the salt of the earth. We have been redeemed from the curse of the law due to Christ's finished works.

Thankful for Choices—
I Choose to Live!

MONICA MONK OLIVER

"Beloved, I pray that you may prosper in all things and be in health, just as your soul prospers."

—3 John 1:2 (NKJV)

We are mere humans. Yes, I am, and you are too. We are wonderfully and beautifully made, with the damages associated with mortality. I experienced human fragilities like secrecy, isolation, and depression. The opportunity to work as an educator had its highs and lows, and they were taking a toll on me. Each day the demands became greater. More and more often the days ended with me in the bed with a migraine. At first, I attributed the painful headaches to long days and nights reading emails, mentally crafting written responses to emails, and writing reports. These were normal obligations for teachers. Teaching is a science and an art. It is a unique mixture of classroom management, covering curricula, identifying learning differences, and providing family counseling. It is both fulfilling and draining, which can negatively affect your health.

Everyone has an example of one person who worked themselves to death. My mother's sister was a true helper and caregiver. She kept up with family members and bought everyone gifts. She worked at the Veterans Affairs Hospital and operated halfway houses for people in recovery. One evening while facilitating a recovery group, my aunt suddenly had a stroke and died. She had a beautiful funeral service. People spoke highly of her and told inspirational stories about her. It was standing room only. However, she died a premature death at the age of 48. As I thought of her, my migraine intensified, and I finally decided to go to the emergency room. I wondered, "Should I call an ambulance to pick me up?" I decided not to because I had not met my insurance deductible and did not want to come out of pocket $500 for a 15-minute ride up to Medical City. Then I wondered, "Should I ask someone to drive me? Who?" I did not want to worry my family. Did I want people in my business? Finally, I decided to keep everyone out of my personal affairs, save money, and drive myself to the hospital. Within hours, I returned home with the reassurance that I was not having a stroke or an aneurysm. I rested for a few hours then conducted my typical routine—wake up, say a prayer, feed my new puppy, squeeze in a physical activity, and begin the day.

As many of us know, teaching is a profession and a calling. It is never boring, the laugh value is priceless, and I enjoy it! This particular school year stretched me beyond my professional experience or any professional development workshop I had ever attended. The physical, emotional, and social challenges of my students' health conditions, their changing family structures, and the assistant teacher's living situation all hit me at once. Those issues demanded that I perform above a teacher's job description. I figured my faith was being tested, so I dug up the old What Would Jesus Do? Pray Until Something Happens bracelets and kept going as I had always done over the years.

The requirements and expectations of this particular school year were steadily increasing. A clear shift in parenting style had occurred. They all wanted test scores proving their child was a gifted and talented student who performed above grade average, scored within a certain percentile, would be accepted into the best private independent school, and was destined to go to an Ivy League university. Few parents wanted to hear that their child loves coming to school, learns, works hard, and is a good person who also scores in the same percentile as most students the same age in the United States. Most parents would rather hear that their child had an academic or psychological diagnosis than to be told their child was an average student.

Every afternoon, I went home exhausted and laid on the couch with a terrible migraine. One day, I suddenly lost the feeling on the right side of my face and in my right leg. A friend who had talked me into starting the process of buying my condo lived nearby. But, my place resembled a single woman's apartment midweek, which is code for messy, so there was no way I was going to call her for help! I managed to put my dog, Little Bit, in her crate and drove myself to the emergency room again.

My vitals were that of a morbidly obese American woman, with the typical statistics and recommendations that come with it. The medical staff was so kind. They treated me like a potential stroke victim. The nurse asked the routine questions. I answered them while mentioning my profession and adding that this year had an unusual amount of stress. The nurse listened carefully. She stated that the work-related stress and perhaps the depression were understandable. However, it did not explain the tingling on the side of my body or the right side of my face and my right leg going numb. Soon afterwards, a person walked in with a needle. Do you know the person wanted to stick the needle in my back? I thought, "WTF?" My worry was for naught. Being morbidly obese, I was too overweight for the needle to reach the proper place for the nurse to conduct the procedure. There are no words to describe the embarrassment and relief I felt. They gave me some liquid Ibuprofen and a referral for an MRI.

Time passed and waking up was a chore. Each morning the birds were chirping in the wrong key, the sun's rays were a dull, dirty yellow and the smell of my favorite comforter caused me to sneeze repeatedly. Plus, the dog was not a real Chihuahua, she was a mutt. In other words, I was depressed. Also, for some reason migraines and fatigue were ever-present. The level of pain had to be God telling me that perhaps I should, kind of, maybe consider stepping out of the boat a little bit. At work, I had some off days saved up and decided to use them to do some soul searching. During this time, the right side of my body went numb. I had to brace myself against the wall in order to stand. The numbness passed, but it really scared me. I contacted my primary care physician whom I trusted and felt comfortable sharing my life's details.

She had been my doctor since she opened her practice. That day, our conversation ended with me crying uncontrollably. She told me to make the appointment immediately for an MRI. Noticeably, she did not engage in casual conversation as usual; instead, she was all business and encouraged me to review my health insurance policy and to take care of business matters. She also told me not to do one thing. Of course, I only did the one thing I was instructed not to do. I Googled my symptoms and self-diagnosed.

After one week of Google research, I narrowed my condition down to about three different illnesses. By this time, I had lost much of the feeling in both of my legs. While I was sitting on the couch wearing circulation stockings and thinking to myself, "How could I let my health get so out of hand?" my dear friend, who is also a physician, called me. In her usual greeting she asked, "Hey, Little Magic, what's going on?"

"Nothing, but I think I have diabetes or something," I said.

"When did they diagnose you?" she questioned.

I sighed, "They haven't, and I can't figure out what's wrong."

"Uhh, you should go get an MRI," she suggested.

I took her advice, scheduled an appointment, and went for the procedure. They did not find anything. The same day, they injected me with dye and performed the procedure again. Later, I met with the doctor to review the results. He pulled out a printed image of my brain, pointed to the lesions and said, "You have multiple sclerosis."

I sat there with the results. We talked about some of the common symptoms: tingling, numbness, tremors, headaches, and difficulty walking. All of which I had been experiencing. Immediately, I thought of the ending of Richard Pryor's life. The doctor recalled some of Richard Pryor's work, repeated some of his inappropriate jokes, and summed up his life. Then he asked me, "Have you lived the kind of life Richard Pryor lived?"

"Well, no," I answered.

"Then you probably won't experience the illness like he experienced it," the doctor replied with a caring grin. MS is different for everyone." He wrote a referral for a neurologist and wished me well.

I eventually found a physician. She performed a neurological exam, prescribed Copaxone injections, and suggested a support group. Being in a support group was quite the experience. We were a diverse group from different backgrounds all with similar questions. What in the world did having multiple sclerosis mean exactly for all of us? During these meetings, I learned that people with MS live a normal life span. To my surprise, I also learned that MS medication without insurance can cost over $2,000 monthly. Many patients experience moments of financial ruin, having to choose between paying mortgage, buying food, or paying for medication. It was during these meetings that people shared information about assistance programs, guidelines to answering certain criterion questions, experiences with job discrimination, supporting the Americans with Disabilities Act, the best places on the body for injections, and how to skip days to help stretch the medication when one is in a financial pinch and cannot afford medication.

I continued my regular activities, kept the diagnosis a secret, and hid the symptoms. Meanwhile, absolutely nothing was going right. I struggled personally, professionally, and spiritually. Stress and depression worsened multiple sclerosis' effect on me. I was trapped in a vicious cycle. As I tried to hide the illness, the frequency of my relapses increased, and my symptoms intensified. I was struggling to complete my job responsibilities while living a poor quality of life. I finally hit the proverbial wall and crashed. It was exactly what I needed.

I chose to disclose my health condition to close family and friends. They all responded the same way and said, "I knew it was something, I just didn't want to be nosey. I didn't want to say anything."

When you notice people struggling, please ask them if they are ok and if they need or want help. Most of the time, people are waiting and want someone to reach out to them.

My family and friends, which are synonymous to me, were so supportive. Eventually, I faced one of my last fears by sharing my health condition with my school administrators. I continued attending the support group and signed up for National Multiple Sclerosis Society, Walk MS: Dallas. My family, friends, and many teachers and administrators signed up to join the walk team. Why had I chosen to try to face this condition alone?

Continuing to manage my illness, I settled into acceptance. I committed to learning more about MS (i.e., how it affects my life, signs of relapse, and how to recognize self-inflicted triggers). My close family and friends also learned how to identify warning signs and had my permission to speak freely in order to help me. Even my "chimutt," Little Bit, learned to sense early onsets of MS relapses. I read and studied my insurance coverage. If the time comes, I know the steps to take to order cooling devices, walking assistance equipment, and in-home short term and long-term care. I am not claiming any of this; however, I live in full knowledge of the condition. I am aware of the prognosis of multiple sclerosis and I understand that the symptoms are unpredictable. So, even though I am not scared anymore, should I simply wander through life and see what happens? No!

One night, while watching a YouTube clip of *The Curious Case of Benjamin Button*, I resolved to live with intention. I am a person of faith who believes in and has witnessed the healing power of Jesus Christ. I decided to work to become the best version of me, beginning with my emotional well-being. I found a psychologist who shared my belief. The first thing he did was help me to understand the purpose and benefit of setting healthy boundaries. He also encouraged me to join a support group. This time, I followed doctors' orders. Not just his, but orders from my primary care physician, neurologist, and pastor as well.

SOUL REFLECTION:
I learned to be authentic, to understand God's grace, and to extend it to others. I choose to live with intention, to take care of my physical and spiritual health, to value my time, and to reserve the right to start all over again. At times, it

has been hard to rebuild bridges, eat more than a couple slices of humble pie, and be rejected. However, with each step (even if it is a misstep), I am thankful to be able to keep moving, revisit old goals, rediscover passions, and embark on new adventures!

Sources

Unless otherwise indicated, scripture quotations are from the Holy Bible, King James Version. All rights reserved.

Scriptures marked NASB are taken from the New American Standard Bible®. Copyright © 1960, 1962, 1963, 1968, 1971, 1972, 1973, 1975, 1977, 1995 by The Lockman Foundation. Used by permission.

Scriptures marked NIV are taken from the New International Version®. Copyright © 1973, 1978, 1984, 2011 by Biblica, Inc.™. All rights reserved.

Scriptures marked NKJV are taken from the New King James Version®. Copyright © 1982 by Thomas Nelson. All rights reserved.

Scriptures marked ESV are taken from English Standard Version®. Copyright © 2001 by Crossway, a publishing ministry of Good News Publishers. All rights reserved.

Scriptures marked MSG are taken from The Message®. Copyright © 1993, 1994, 1995, 1996, 2000, 2001, 2002. Used by permission of NavPress Publishing Group.

Scriptures marked CEB are taken from Common English Bible. All rights reserved

About the Authors

Rev. Dr. Terry Richardson has served as the senior pastor of the First Baptist Church, South Orange, New Jersey, since 1997. He earned both his master of divinity and doctor of ministry degrees from New Brunswick Theological Seminary (NBTS), New Brunswick, New Jersey, with a concentration in metro-urban ministry. He worked as an adjunct professor at Essex County College and is a recipient of numerous awards and recognitions including those from Phi Delta Kappa, Inc., the NAACP, Christian Talk Radio, Essex County Prosecutor, and the National Organization of Black Law Enforcement Executives.

Dr. Richardson has sat on numerous community boards and is active locally and nationally on matters of social justice. He is married to NaDeen Bridgforth Richardson. Together they are the proud parents of four adult children: Shannon, Deven, Kayla, and Jeremiah.

Alicia Simon's growth in business and her passion for serving others has helped her coach women who are stuck (just like she was) toward spiritual transformation, vibrant health, and financial freedom.

Alicia diligently helps families develop **Nourished** bodies by teaching them to seek natural health solutions using essential oils. She coaches women to become financially **Empowered** by giving themselves permission to actively pursue their purpose and build thriving businesses while successfully mommying.

Alicia has been married to Wadell Simon for 12 years and they have six beautiful children, ages two to twenty-six. Together, Alicia and Wadell fervently encourage others to seek transformation and move toward **Whole** life living by sharing their faith walk publicly on several social media platforms. Connect with Alicia and let her help you begin to create a N.E.W. life today!

Learn more at www.aliciasimonlive.com

Debbie Chandler is a restoration life coach, support group facilitator, speaker, and author. But, most importantly, she is a survivor. Debbie is a firm believer that God gives his toughest battles to His strongest Soldiers, as her life and path to happiness has been nothing short of a battle. Debbie survived tragedies such as: sexual abuse, domestic violence, depression, abortion, multiple suicide attempts, and substance abuse. However, she has resolved to live as a victor, never a victim!

Through the grace of God, Debbie is also chronicling part of her life story and testimony in her soon to be released book, *A Double Portion of Grace, Part One: Overcoming the Guilt & Shame of Sexual Violations*. A prayer warrior and lifelong fighter, Debbie is passionate about positively encouraging, uplifting, and empowering others with her story.

Learn more at www.coachdebbiechandler.com

Kymberli Williams is a native of Charleston, West Virginia. A strong proponent for women in business, Kymberli is an entrepreneur and business owner who started her own company in 2017 as a virtual/personal assistant after a career as a paralegal and c-level executive assistant. Kymberli's company, WMS Virtual Assist, LLC is the perfect cost-effective staffing solution for busy companies, law firms, entrepreneurs, start-ups, and individuals or families in need of virtual assistance. Kymberli attended college preparatory school in Tyrone, Pennsylvania, and college at Marshall University in Huntington, West Virginia.

Kymberli has one son, Derek Chandler Jordan, and refers to him as God's gift and saving grace for the entirety of her adult life. Through struggles and sacrifices, Kymberli has a love of people from all walks of life and plans to fulfill her destiny solely under God's direction.

To connect, email her at wmsvirtualassist@gmail.com

Cynthia Fox Everett is a mother of four and a grandmother of seven. A US Army Veteran of 14 years, Cynthia has an associate's degree in criminal justice/protective services. She furthered her education at Shaw University.

In 2003, Cynthia rededicated her life to Christ and accepted the mission and responsibility to serve in the house of the Lord. Her desire is to make a difference in the lives of others, especially fellow Veterans. She is also dedicated to inspiring others to seek Jesus and find the strength to heal so that they can have the courage to rewrite their future, tell their story, and help others heal. Cynthia strives to love others unconditionally and to teach others how to love themselves so that they can feel and know genuine love.

A certified life coach, Cynthia is also a coauthor of the Amazon bestseller *Souled Out* with visionary author, Cheryl Polote-Williamson.

To connect, email her at invisible2visible18@gmail.com

Christine Norman believes that faith is not just for Sundays; we live what we truly believe every moment of every day. She created LYFE365 to help people of faith live in faith every day. As a minister, writer, and speaker, Christine preaches, teaches classes, writes curriculums, and facilitates workshops for women, couples, and teens.

Christine holds a bachelor's degree in human services/management, a master of Christian ministry degree with an emphasis in leadership from Liberty Theological Seminary, and she is currently completing a master of counseling degree at the Townsend Institute of Leadership and Counseling at Concordia University, all aimed at helping others live and lead better.

Despite her academic training, Christine feels nothing in life qualifies her for the call of God except His amazing love and unyielding grace. Christine wears many hats, but her favorites include wife, mother, friend, and woman after God's own heart.

Learn more at www.LYFE365.com

Kimberly Solomon has endured many trials but is still standing. She is anointed to speak and minister to women of all ages, races, and religious backgrounds.

Her journey of looking for love in some of the most tumultuous places has taught her how to live life in high definition. She is happily married to Keith. They are certified neuro-linguistic practitioners, Amazon bestselling authors of five books, and they have eight children.

Kimberly has honorably served for over 18 years in the Air Force and earned her bachelor's degrees in IT and business marketing. She is also a licensed esthetician, helping women be their best from the inside out.

Kimberly is an extremely talented liturgical dancer and sought-after choreographer. Her purpose, mission, and goal in life is to help as many people as she can. All that God has poured into Kimberly, she vows to pour into others.

Learn more at www.keepersinternational.org

Sharon L. Graves is an entrepreneur and founder of Empower2Build! Inc., a 501(c)(3) non-profit organization partnering with facilities, communities, and institutions to empower individuals, families, and communities. Sharon is also a servant, encourager, inspirer, exhorter, life and personal development coach, minister of the Gospel, and elder/overseer at Word of Life Empowerment Ministries International.

Sharon holds a master of arts in biblical counseling, a bachelor of science in psychology: Christian counseling, and she is also a credentialed global career development facilitator.

As one with a heart for God's people, church, and marketplace ministry, it is Sharon's desire to assist and minister (by way of the Holy Spirit) to areas of brokenness and fragility of heart, mind, and spirit. Sharon aims to impact and empower lives using training and development methods as well as practical and spiritual techniques so that people may breakthrough, overcome, and walk in their God-purposed liberty and life.

To connect, email her at sharon.graves@ymail.com

Sheila Malloy-Hall is the founder of Healing 2 Grace, Inc., a non-profit organization addressing the impact and aftermath of abuse and domestic violence. Championing women to reach their highest level of internal fulfillment, Sheila shares how she survived mental, physical, sexual, and emotional abuses and prompts her audience to begin their healing journey. Her dynamic message inspires her audiences to reach a place of hope and unbounding joy.

Sheila helps women demolish the barriers and destroy the lie of the enemy that says, "You will live forever with the pain." By getting the conversation started, she challenges her audiences to change the way they talk about abuse. Sheila's deep-seated passion is to be a role model as she shares her survivor strategies to empower women, increase their self-worth, and evoke their desire to be free from abuse!

Learn more at www.healing2grace.org

Laquita Hogan is an author, certified credit counselor, and professional tax advisor. She is the co-owner of First Step Tax Services. Laquita holds a degree in mass communications journalism.

Laquita developed a sense of mastery for writing at a very young age. She currently writes poetry for special occasions, previously worked as editor-in-chief for the school newspaper at Dallas County Community College Districts, wrote for the former online magazine, FORMation, and currently holds the position of managing editor for the local dance team, Elev8ed Elites.

Laquita hopes not only to continue helping others with financial literacy, but to start an online greeting card business for the urban community. With God's direction, Laquita desires to inspire others with her writing.

Laquita currently resides in Lewisville, Texas, with her husband, Marquis, and three daughters, Shakeyra, Neveah, and Ma'Kayla.

Learn more at www.mahoganyspeaks.com

Sonya Scott is a lover and servant of God. She is also an author, blogger, workplace consultant, and the founder of Professional POP, a faith-based organization whose mission is to support and assist professionals through Scripture, prayer, community, and biblical application. Sonya is an advocate for individuals realizing and pursuing their professional purpose by utilizing their God-given gifts while understanding the concept and importance of serving God in their profession.

Sonya serves on the advisory board for CircularFlo, LLC, a mentoring organization focused on connecting women to their purpose through faith, leadership, and outreach.

A native of Detroit, Michigan, Sonya currently resides in the Dallas-Fort Worth area and is a member of One Community Church in Plano, Texas, where she serves in the couples and women's ministries.

Sonya and her husband, Imara, have been married for 21 years and are blessed with two sons, DeVaughn and Donovan Scott.

Learn more at www.thepopsuite.com

Windi Floyd Reynolds is the author of the book, *To Raya with Love,* and the owner of Focused Ink Group LLC. An Indie Author Legacy Awards nominee, Windi's journey as an author began in 2017, but her dream of becoming a writer has been a lifetime goal. "Focused plans lead to a focused journey," is the mission statement of Windi and Focused Ink. Through journaling with Focused Ink, Windi hopes to reach the world and inspire others to pursue their dreams.

Windi is a two-time graduate of Savannah State University and a certified healthcare leader at one of the largest healthcare facilities in Savannah, Georgia, where she resides. She also has roots in Miami, Florida.

Learn more at www.focusedink.com

DeNesha Manning is a gifted communicator with experience in entrepreneurship, acting, modeling, and writing. She is a Veteran of the United States Army National Guard. Her educational background includes a bachelor of science degree from the University of Central Arkansas, as well as, an MBA from Belhaven University.

With over 11 years of corporate experience, DeNesha exceeded goals while maximizing portfolios consisting of multi-billion-dollar product lines in the healthcare industry. DeNesha is a gifted leader and a change agent who believes in leadership, integrity, and creating an atmosphere built on trust, understanding, creativity, and development.

DeNesha is a seeker of wisdom and a kingdom representative. Her brand, Designed to Rule, embodies her company's vision: "To help people discover their gifts, maximize their potential, and serve their unique specialization to the world." Her company, Fashioned4Dominion, LLC is on a mission to stop the disease of settling for less from spreading.

Learn more at www.fashioned4dominion.org

Winifred "Teddi" Jones is a woman of God who is a mother of two, Keldrick: 30 and Kiara: 26, and a grandmother of two, Kaiden: 5 and King: 3; all four are her pride and joy. Winifred has spent the last 31 years doing what she loves—helping others as a nurse. She is currently working toward her nurse practitioner/MSN degree and plans to open her own practice and counseling center.

Winifred also wears many hats as a praise dancer, Vacation Bible School teacher, and choreographer. She currently works at Faith Presbyterian Hospice where she volunteers after hours as a bereavement facilitator for children. Her goals are to birth her first novel and nurture her entrepreneurial spirit.

Winifred, a native Texan, is an avid sports fan who enjoys traveling, learning new languages, shopping for shoes, going to amusement parks and the theatre, and listening to all genres of music.

LaShonda Davison is a mother of two beautiful children, Amber and Carl. She is engaged to Brian McCaskill, a wonderful, God-fearing, loving, and hard-working man. They reside in the beautiful sunshine state of Florida where you couldn't ask for more perfect weather outside of the Caribbean.

LaShonda is a child of God, a mother, an event planner, and a politician. She wears many hats on different days and sometimes you may catch her wearing them all at once. Some people ask her how she does it. She simply says, "That's what the Lord created the woman for, to multitask. Right?"

LaShonda grew up a Navy brat, which caused her to basically grow up around the world. She is a big advocate for children's education. Her passion is helping others. One of her mottos is: "Sit still, be silent, and let God work it out."

Learn more at www.lashondamdavison.com

LaVerne M. Perlie is a dynamic wife, mother, daughter, ordained clergy, nurse, author, and inspirational speaker. Her passion is encouraging and inspiring women and children, through her testimony, to have an improved quality of life despite experiencing relentless challenges.

LaVerne enjoys serving others, watching lives transform, and building partnerships in her community. She is the executive director and founder of Flame of Fire Ministries, a 501(c)(3) organization, servicing women and at-risk youth. Flame of Fire Ministries provides workforce development training for women recovering from addiction, and college preparation, scholarships, mentoring, and leadership development for middle and high school aged males.

LaVerne is also an evangelist who develops evangelism plans for urban communities, coordinates discipleship classes, and oversees the strategic plans for several church ministries.

Learn more at https://badzherstory.com

Katherine Romar is an aspiring freelance writer and poet. She served in the armed forces for 20 years and traveled throughout her career as a Soldier experiencing life but aspiring to be a bestselling author.

Katherine writes to encourage and strengthen all who read her story. She is an active minister and advocate for God.

Katherine retired and lives in Killen, Texas, with her husband, Kirk. Her first novel will soon be published.

To connect, email her at baileyromar@yahoo.com

Dionne Selby is a certified life coach and owner of Perfectly Flawed, LLP. She has a love for her family as well as a passion for educating people in the community. Her aspiration is to help others to always see the greatness in themselves.

Dionne is a wife, mother, and manager in the banking industry. She is also a graduate of East Carolina University with a bachelor of science in business education. She holds over 10 years' experience in development, management, coaching, marriage, and motherhood.

Dionne's gift is to help motivate others to accomplish their relationship, personal development, finance, health, and wellness goals. Her mission is to empower people with a new outlook, helping them to create the life they desire.

Learn more at www.iamperfectlyflawed.com

Dana Campbell is a hard-working, spiritual, friendly, adventurous, positive, compassionate, and devoted mother of three young, energetic children. She is currently the director of a well-respected education and training non-profit organization for adults and young girls.

Dana has a master's of science in human services with over 12 years' experience in workforce skills training and disability programming for adults, helping them to realize their potential and become contributing citizens in their community through education and training. Dana also volunteers at her church as a co-leader of the Diamonds WESS Group (Women's Empowerment Support Group) and Toastmasters International. Both groups are dedicated to empowering, uplifting, and supporting men and women.

Dana desires success while helping people become their best self through self-compassion, prayer, and devotion to God. Her ambition is to become an entrepreneur. Dana currently resides in Maryland.

To connect, email her at makemoments4u@gmail.com

Angela T. Kinnel is an 11-year veteran educator, minister, author, and public speaker. A native of Dawson, Georgia, she is the only daughter of three children born to Edward Kinnel, Sr. and the late Stella W. Kinnel. Angela earned a bachelor of science degree in agricultural economics from Fort Valley State University and went on to pursue a master of science degree in the same area at Tuskegee University.

After entering the field of education, Angela obtained a master of arts degree in education with an emphasis in curriculum and instruction. She is also a 2017 graduate of World Changers Bible School where she earned an associate degree in Christian studies. As a student, Angela coauthored her first book.

Angela is a member of World Changers Church International in College Park, Georgia. She is also an active member of Delta Sigma Theta Sorority, Incorporated.

Monica Monk Oliver is a seasoned educator whose credentials span from international certifications to using her hands-on approach when working with families, organizations, and individuals. After earning a master's in counseling, she studied abroad at the Centro Internazionale Studi Montessoriani in Bergamo, Italy. Subsequently, Monica was personally invited by the founder and executive director of the Montessori Model United Nations to participate in their teacher and leadership training. She gained a global perspective of education through these combined experiences. Aside from teaching, Monica is recognized as a consultant and administrator with experiences in both the United States and Canada. She is dedicated to researching, learning, and implementing best practices to help children and to assist their families.

Monica supports organizations that empower communities through education, job training, and advocacy. She is a longtime team captain and participant in the National Multiple Sclerosis Society, Walk MS: Dallas.

Nationally acclaimed bestselling author, transformational speaker, and success coach **Cheryl Polote-Williamson** has established multiple platforms, dedicating her consulting practice to cultivate innovative business solutions, strategic marketing initiatives, and financial acumen for entrepreneurs. A global leader, Cheryl is the CEO and founder of Williamson Media Group, LLC, and Cheryl Polote-Williamson, LLC, where her knowledge and expertise are used as a conduit to affirm others in pursuit of their purpose.

Cheryl's unmatched credibility in the industry has earned her numerous awards, including the Chocolate Social Award for best online community, the Dallas Top 25 Award, and the Female Success Factor Award. She has been named amongst the Who's Who In Black Dallas Publishing, held a position on the Forbes Coaches Council, and participates in the NAACP Author Pavilion, the Congressional Black Caucus, Christian Women in Media, and the National Association of Women Business Owners.

A prolific author and winner of the 2017 Indie Author Legacy Awards, Cheryl has published multiple books, including Soul Reborn, Words from the Spirit for the 289

Spirit, Safe House, Affirmed, Soul Talk, Soul Bearer, Soul Source, and The Success Factor, with more titles on the way. She is also producing a play entitled Soul Purpose, set for a 2018 debut.

Cheryl and her husband, Russell, currently reside in Flower Mound, Texas. They have three beautiful children, Russell Jr., Lauren, and Courtney, as well as an adorable granddaughter, Leah. In her spare time, Cheryl enjoys traveling, reading, serving others, and spending quality time with family and friends.

To learn more, visit her website at
www.cherylpwilliamson.com

CREATING DISTINCTIVE BOOKS WITH INTENTIONAL RESULTS

We're a collaborative group of creative masterminds with a mission to produce high-quality books to position you for monumental success in the marketplace.

Our professional team of writers, editors, designers, and marketing strategists work closely together to ensure that every detail of your book is a clear representation of the message in your writing.

Want to know more?
Write to us at info@publishyourgift.com
or call (888) 949-6228

Discover great books, exclusive offers, and more at
www.PublishYourGift.com

Connect with us on social media

@publishyourgift

www.ingramcontent.com/pod-product-compliance
Lightning Source LLC
Chambersburg PA
CBHW071321110526
44591CB00010B/971